Past Masters
General Editor Keith T

Mendel

CW00969513

Past Masters

AQUINAS Anthony Kenny
ARISTOTLE Jonathan Barnes
BACH Denis Arnold
FRANCIS BACON Anthony Quinton
BAYLE Elisabeth Labrousse
BERKELEY J. O. Urmson
THE BUDDHA Michael Carrithers
BURKE C. B. Macpherson
CARLYLE A. L. Le Quesne
CHAUCER George Kane
CLAUSEWITZ Michael Howard
COBBETT Raymond Williams
COLERIDGE Richard Holmes
CONFUCIUS Raymond Dawson
DANTE George Holmes
DARWIN Jonathan Howard
DIDEROT Peter France
GEORGE ELIOT Rosemary Ashton
ENGELS Terrell Carver
GALILEO Stillman Drake

GOETHE T. J. Reed
HEGEL Peter Singer
HOMER Jasper Griffin
HUME A. J. Ayer
JESUS Humphrey Carpenter
KANT Roger Scruton
LAMARCK L. J. Jordanova
LEIBNIZ G. MacDonald Ross
LOCKE John Dunn
MACHIAVELLI Quentin Skinner
MARX Peter Singer
MENDEL Vítězslav Orel
MONTAIGNE Peter Burke
THOMAS MORE Anthony Kenny
WILLIAM MORRIS Peter Stansky
MUHAMMAD Michael Cook
NEWMAN Owen Chadwick
PASCAL Alban Krailsheimer
PETRARCH Nicholas Mann
PLATO R. M. Hare
PROUST Derwent May
TOLSTOY Henry Gifford

Forthcoming

AUGUSTINE Henry Chadwick
BERGSON Leszek Kolakowski
JOSEPH BUTLER R. G. Frey
CERVANTES P. E. Russell
COPERNICUS Owen Gingerich
DESCARTES Tom Sorell
DISRAELI John Vincent
ERASMUS James McConica
GIBBON J. W. Burrow
GODWIN Alan Ryan
HERZEN Aileen Kelly
JEFFERSON Jack P. Greene
JOHNSON Pat Rogers
KIERKEGAARD Patrick Gardiner
LEONARDO E. H. Gombrich

LINNAEUS W. T. Stearn
MILL William Thomas
MONTESQUIEU Judith Shklar
NEWTON P. M. Rattansi
ROUSSEAU Robert Wokler
RUSKIN George P. Landow
RUSSELL John G. Slater
SHAKESPEARE Germaine Greer
ADAM SMITH D. D. Raphael
SOCRATES Bernard Williams
SPINOZA Roger Scruton
VICO Peter Burke
VIRGIL Jasper Griffin
WYCLIF Anthony Kenny

and others

Vítězslav Orel

Mendel

Translated by Stephen Finn

Oxford   New York

OXFORD UNIVERSITY PRESS

1984

Oxford University Press, Walton Street, Oxford OX2 6DP

London New York Toronto
Delhi Bombay Calcutta Madras Karachi
Kuala Lumpur Singapore Hong Kong Tokyo
Nairobi Dar es Salaam Cape Town
Melbourne Auckland

and associated companies in
Beirut Berlin Ibadan Mexico City Nicosia

Oxford is a trade mark of Oxford University Press

First published 1984 as an Oxford University Press paperback
and simultaneously in a hardback edition

British Library Cataloguing in Publication Data

Orel, Vítězslav
Mendel.—(Past Masters)
1. Mendel, Gregor Johann   2. Genetics—History—19th century
I. Title   II. Series
575.1'092'4   QH31.M45
ISBN 0-19-287625-2
ISBN 0-19-287624-4 Pbk

Library of Congress Cataloging in Publication Data

Orel, Vítězslav.
Mendel.
(Past Masters)
Bibliography: p.
Includes index.
1. Mendel, Gregor, 1822–1884.   2.Geneticists—Austria
—Biography.   I. Title.   II. Series.
QH31.M4506813 1984 575.1'1'0924 [B]   84–10089
ISBN 0-19-287625-2
ISBN 0-19-287624-4 (pbk.)

Set by Hope Services, Abingdon
Printed in Great Britain by
Cox & Wyman Ltd, Reading

Contents

List of illustrations

Introduction

A special place is reserved in the annals of science for a select few—those of whom it can be said that their work has radically changed man's understanding of the universe and of himself, and revolutionised human thought. On that roll of honour, with names such as Nicolaus Copernicus, Isaac Newton and Charles Darwin, is that of the man whose research laid the foundations of the central biological science, genetics. Gregor Mendel's experiments on plant hybridisation and the theory he created to explain their results reshaped scientific attitudes not only to heredity, but to nearly all the phenomena of the living world. Nevertheless, Mendel had been dead for sixteen years before his name began to appear on the pages of the world's scientific press, when his research work was dramatically 'rediscovered'.

Mendel first presented an account of his ten years of experiments with plant hybrids in 1865. He read his paper at the February and March meetings of the Natural Science Society of Brno (formerly Brünn in Moravia, part of the Habsburg Monarchy; now in Czechoslovakia). The next year it was published, in German, in the society's proceedings, and sent to 133 other associations of natural scientists in a number of different countries. The response it drew from Mendel's contemporaries was minimal. It was not until 1900 that, within the space of two months, three more papers were published, describing virtually the same results. Their authors, Hugo de Vries, Carl Correns and Erich von Tschermak, had worked independently, in Amsterdam, Tübingen and

Vienna respectively. All three candidly admitted having been preceded by several decades by a little-known monk working in Brno. Thus the year 1900 is regarded as the starting-point of the science of heredity.

The question of heredity had aroused man's interest since ancient times, for its effects were to be seen among his own kind and in the animals he kept and the crops he grew, wherever members of the same species exhibited different physical characteristics. Such characteristics, which biologists call *traits* or *characters*, could be qualitative, such as the colour of the eye, or of blossom; or quantitative, such as a man's height, an animal's growth-rate, or the number of grains in an ear of corn. It was evident from early on that the organisms of the present generation owed such characters to their parents, or to more remote ancestors. But it was not understood why parents having, say, differing eye-colour might have one child with the character of the father and another with that of the mother. Very often the child's characters seemed to be the product of both parental traits, blended together.

As it was gradually realised that the characters of an organism were influenced by the environment, particularly by nutritional and climatic conditions, the phenomenon began to seem increasingly complex. When man first learned to cultivate plants and to keep domestic animals it must have been observed that some organisms which had desirable characters tended to pass these on to the next generation, along with undesirable characters. Man began to select animals and plants for reproduction and gradually he created new, more efficient plant varieties and more useful animal breeds. Later he even learned to cross animals with different desirable characters to achieve new combinations of them. Towards the end of the eighteenth century, pioneer animal breeders were concerned to understand how characters were inherited, but it remained frustratingly clear that, despite the fact that 'like begets like', it was also true that 'like begets unlike'.

Following the discovery of sexual organisation in plants, eighteenth-century naturalists began to experiment with artificial plant fertilisation and observed the transfer of individual characters from generation to generation. At the beginning of the nineteenth century an effort was made to discover the underlying principles of heredity. Many different hypotheses were advanced. They can be grouped into those which assumed that one sex, male or female, solely or predominantly determines the heredity, and those which assumed that both parents contribute to the hereditary make-up of the offspring.

Darwin, in his study of the evolutionary process, collected a vast amount of information on animal and plant breeding, including the results of plant hybridisation, and also performed experiments of his own. Yet in his masterpiece, *On the Origin of Species* (1859), he came to the conclusion that 'the laws governing inheritance are for the most part unknown.'

As the first copies of Darwin's book came off the press, the enigma of heredity was already receiving the careful attention of Gregor Mendel. His precursors in research into plant hybridisation had investigated parental plants differing in many characters. Considering the plant as a whole, they tended to see a blending of parental types in the hybrids, and were unable to find any pattern in the transfer of heredity. Mendel, performing experiments with edible peas as a model plant, had a novel approach to the problem. He crossed two pure-breeding varieties of peas which differed from one another only in clear-cut and easily distinguishable alternative discrete characters. Thus he reduced the problem of analysing hereditary transmission to the simplest possible terms; and he was able to show that all hybrids acquired the same characters from their parents. He then fertilised hybrid plants with their own pollen, and proved that in the next generation both characters of the parental plants reappeared. Adducing a large number of observations, he was able to illustrate the segregation of parental characters in a constant ratio, $3:1$. In other words, the parental characters not exhibited in the hybrids reappeared in subsequent generations, as did the characters of the hybrids themselves. Mendel's conclusion was that the transfer of characters is governed by their determinants through the germ cells and that these determinants combined in accordance with the statistical law of chance. They remained discrete; they did not blend.

So, rather as Copernicus had rejected the ancient idea of a geocentric universe, Mendel overthrew the age-old and still prevailing notion of blending inheritance and introduced a new concept: that of investigating the inheritance of discrete characters as they appeared in parents and offspring. He thus laid the foundation of a new science, christened by William Bateson in 1906 genetics. Mendel's theory is also called corpuscular because hereditary determinants, later (in 1909) called *genes*, were conceived by him as minute concrete bodies.

Thanks to Bateson, an English translation of Mendel's paper appeared in 1901, prompting translation into other languages. This in turn led to a surge of interest in further research into heredity. This research, into not only plants but also animals and man himself, carried out by biologists in many countries, led to further revelations concerning the principles of heredity. After the first decade of the century, the pattern of inheritance first demonstrated for seven characters in peas by Mendel, and subsequently generalised to other species and other characters, was usually referred to as Mendel's Laws of Heredity.

In 1904 Bateson went to Brno, wishing to see for himself the scene of Mendel's experiments, but was disappointed to find very little information other than the published paper itself. It was at about that time that the first biographical studies on Mendel as a pioneer scientist began to appear, though there was pitifully little information to go on. But Bateson's visit to Brno led to the discovery and preservation of documents relating to Mendel, and from 1906 a small Mendel museum was gradually built up in the Augustinian monastery. It was not until 1924, however, that H. Iltis, a teacher of natural history in Brno, used the material (some collected by himself) for the first extensive biography, published in German in 1924. Though Iltis described briefly the creative cultural milieu of the monastery and the enthusiasm of the local natural scientists for research at the time Mendel was doing his work, the view has prevailed in later biographical literature that Mendel arrived at his theory by chance, working alone in the small provincial town of Brno, and that it was this isolation from great scientific centres which accounted for the belated recognition of his work.

The standard version of Mendel's life-story is quickly told. He was born into the family of a Moravian peasant who held his land in feoff. The boy was talented, yet only with help from his parents and with private tutoring was he able to acquire a secondary education. His desire to study further led him to enter the Augustinian monastery in Brno, a well-known centre of learning. After attending the theological seminary in Brno, he was able, with the support of Abbot Napp (1792–1867), to study natural sciences at Vienna University. On his return he became a supply teacher of physics at the Brno Oberrealschule, though he did not manage to pass his teacher's examinations. Mendel brought with him to Brno from his native village an interest in growing plants, which later led him to experiment with their crossing. On evaluating the results of these experiments he discovered the laws of heredity which were later to make him famous. This traditional view of Mendel, as we shall see, seriously underestimates both his achievement itself and the creative environment which engendered it.

After the Second World War, genetical research entered a period of rapid expansion, with biochemists and biophysicists working side by side, and one hundred years after the publication of Mendel's brief report on his findings the first major advances were being made in the field of molecular genetics. Mendel's report, by now considered a classic, had been repeatedly republished in many different languages, and the main principles of his work continued to form the basis of even the most modern research. At the centenary in 1965, geneticists meeting to review the development of genetics and its current teaching began to ask new questions regarding Mendel's work and the circumstances surrounding it. It was suggested that the rules referred to as Mendel's Laws of Heredity were not formulated by Mendel himself, but were read into his work by those who rediscovered it in 1900. After 1965 systematic exploration of the archives was begun, and the new information obtained overthrew the persistent stereotype of Mendel as an unsophisticated empiricist who almost by chance came upon the all-important laws of heredity.

What motivated Mendel's scientific interest in plant breeding and hybridisation? How did he arrive at the constant segregation ratios for the appearance of characters in hybrid progeny? What was his attitude to the evolutionary ideas of the latter half of the last century? How was he able to conduct such exacting experiments in a monastery garden? In order to understand Mendel's enthusiasm for research, and the conditions under which he carried out his experiments and arrived at his theory, we must take a brief look at the intellectual background of his native country and at the growth of scientific ideas at Vienna University. Even as a boy, Mendel was fortunate enough to come into contact with some remarkable men who stimulated his interest in the study of natural sciences. In the Brno monastery he found a centre of creative interest in both science and culture. His enthusiasm was boosted in the revolutionary year 1848: the emperor of the Habsburg Monarchy was forced to convoke the constitutional assembly, which inspired hopes of greater freedom—for the Augustinians in Brno, freedom to pursue scientific and teaching activities. Science was actually encouraged, since it served the interests of the increasingly influential middle classes. This was the environment in which Mendel began to study natural sciences, at first privately in the monastery, and then at Vienna University.

In his research he realised an ambition fully in keeping with the monastery's mission, which, in his view, had always comprised 'the cultivation of science in all its aspects'. Later, Mendel became abbot of the monastery. His new position and changing political circumstances meant that he was unable to devote himself fully to the pursuit of science. He did not even live to see his achievements properly acknowledged. But after 1900 his theory of heredity became part of the mainstream of scientific knowledge, and his name known throughout the civilised world.

1 The intellectual background

In 1806, Christian Carl André (1763–1831) presented the renascent Agricultural Society in Brno with an ambitious programme of economic and social development. He enthusiastically invoked the 'most noble power of science', without which substantial economic and social progress would be impossible, and stressed that advances in mathematics, physics, chemistry and statistics would, together with the other sciences, lead to improvements in agricultural and industrial production techniques, and, moreover, ensure future prosperity by creating new techniques. He referred to the great discoveries of Copernicus and Newton, and also recalled the invention of lightning conductors by Benjamin Franklin (1706–90) and the Moravian Fr. Prokop Diviš (1696–1755). Such examples were intended to encourage members to carry out theoretical research in natural science, although André admitted that the results of such work might well not be apparent until many years later; only then, perhaps, would they win the admiration and gratitude of the civilisation they had benefited. Even now, added André, 'we may be laying the necessary foundations, or we may do so later, without suspecting what success may be in store.' His words were almost prophetic: Mendel's work was to owe a great deal to the interest in natural sciences excited in the province by André.

It was through his interest in the organised promotion of science that André came to Brno in 1798. He was attracted there from Saxony by Moravia's higher level of economic development, and by the activity of private scientific societies there; one of his first contacts was Count Salm-Reifferscheid (1776–1836), who visited England in 1801 with a group of natural scientists wishing to acquaint themselves with progress in science and industry. They were received by the President of the Royal Society, Joseph Banks, who was also noted for his patronage of agricultural science and encouraged pioneer animal and plant breeding.

Salm recognised in André a naturalist of wide education, with a talent for organisation. Together they created the Royal and Imperial Moravian and Silesian Society for the Improvement of Agriculture, Natural Science and Knowledge of the Country (hereafter the Agricultural Society). Mendel was later to hold an important position in this society.

André became an economic adviser to Count Salm and a secretary of the Agricultural Society, and was thus enabled to throw his full weight behind the cause of the development and application of science. The early momentum gained by the industrial and agricultural revolution in Moravia owed much to him. The Brno area became a focus of industry, especially textiles, which meant increased demands on the quantity and quality of wool produced. André looked abroad for his example, taking a great interest in the activities of the Royal Society in London and the French Academy of Sciences in Paris. He intended that the reorganised Agricultural Society should combine the functions of an academy of sciences and of a learned society.

Salm, as André's patron, required him to concentrate his talents on the improvement of wool production. André soon discovered that some Moravian breeders were working on the methods of Robert Bakewell (1725–95), pioneer in breeding new animal strains for meat production in England. André was fascinated by the whole question, and in order to provide an organisational base for the development of scientific sheep breeding, he formed in 1814 a Sheep Breeders' Association within the Agricultural Society. Publishing his views on methods of artificial selection, he repeatedly emphasised that selection was a matter of science, and that it required the exposition of theoretical principles.

Since 1800 the most successful Moravian breeder of wool sheep had been Ferdinand Geisslern (1792–1824), later known as 'the Moravian Bakewell'. The first to write about him was André himself, who later sent his son Rudolf (1792–1825) to study Geisslern's methods of artificial selection. In 1816 Rudolf André published the first textbook on the scientific selection of sheep, which for many years was a handbook for breeders. The new, scientific, approach to artificial selection and heredity brought great economic benefit. In 1810 an English visitor to Brno was astonished to discover that a 'noble' ram could be sold for 500 or sometimes even 3,000 guilders, while a ram from a common herd fetched only five. This gives some indication of the financial motives behind the immense interest in scientific breeding.

Later, André got to hear of methods of breeding fruit trees by artificial pollination which had been successfully developed in England by Thomas Andrew Knight (1759–1838), and in 1816 recommended their introduction into Moravia. In the same year he organised the Pomological Association as a part of the Agricultural Society, making its first task the establishment of nurseries with a large collection of fruit-tree and vine varieties imported from different countries. Following Knight's example, members of the association began to

11

use artificial pollination to obtain new varieties of fruit trees and vines.

A new nursery was also established in the Augustinian monastery at Brno, on the suggestion of the recently elected abbot, F. C. Napp. So great was the new abbot's enthusiasm for pomiculture and viniculture after taking office in 1825 that he wrote a manual on how to grow improved varieties. The nursery was put in the capable hands of Fr. Keller, procurator of the monastery, and in the 1830s an experienced Hungarian wine-grower described it as a research establishment for vine breeding. When in 1843 Mendel entered the Augustinian monastery, Fr. Keller, who was in charge of the novices, was in frequent contact with him.

Success in breeding sheep, fruit trees, and vines led André to consider in 1820 the possibility of exploiting the artificial fertilisation of plants in order to produce new, higher-yielding cereal varieties. In the same year, G. C. L. Hempel published an article in André's journal in which he claimed that artificial fertilisation would one day be used to breed cereals and other plants; it would, he added, first be necessary to discover the law of plant hybridisation. Thus Hempel, on André's initiative, identified a key problem of plant breeding. He had no idea how the problem was to be solved, but Hempel believed that a new type of scientist would emerge to do so, and even predicted what sort of man he would be— someone with a profound knowledge of botany, acute powers of observation, and limitless patience. That man, Gregor Mendel, was born just two years after the article appeared.

The effort to bring agriculture up to date led to the establishment of agricultural schools, and in 1811 natural history and agriculture was introduced into the curriculum of Moravia's university of Olomouc (Olmütz). In 1823 the post of Professor of Agriculture was taken over by J. K. Nestler (1783–1841), who had previously co-operated with André in editing journals, and who took an interest in sheep breeding. In 1829 he published lectures on heredity and the scientific breeding of livestock and crop plants in the Agricultural Society's journal. The subject aroused interest on account of its economic implications and provoked a debate among breeders on the problems of artificial selection and heredity.

In 1836 Professor Nestler was invited to Brno for the annual conference of the Sheep Breeders' Association and asked to outline the further prospects for improving wool production. He was convinced that the question of heredity was the most pressing question in the practice of breeding. By this he meant the theoretical explanation of a phenomenon which remained an enigma to natural scientists. The debate on artificial selection continued. Its participants in Brno, who had some knowledge of scientific literature from other countries, tended to hold the mechanistic view which took living and inorganic matter to be governed by the same laws. Napp, detaching himself from the practical preoccupations of the breeders, pointed out that they had adduced evidence that characters in sheep were not inherited directly. So the crucial questions were, what *is* inherited? and *how* is it inherited? According to Napp, the answers lay in physiological research. He later remarked, in the course of a discussion on the artificial pollination of fruit trees, that a further unknown was the role of chance. These were key problems, and Mendel was later to consider them all in his programme of research.

At that time Napp was also prominent as the successful chairman of the Pomological Association and active on the committee of the Agricultural Society. His enthusiasm for science was soon deployed in training gifted members of the monastic community for scientific work. He also had a hand in ensuring that natural history and agricultural science continued to be taught at the Philosophical Institute in Brno, in 1825. The Institute was administered by the Bishop's Office and after the death of the first professor the bishop took the view that, as the subject was catered for at Olomouc University, there was no need for the vacant chair in Brno to be filled. Napp declared his opposition and succeeded in having F. Diebl (1770–1859) appointed to the post.

Diebl had already published textbooks and articles containing his views on the principles of breeding plants through artificial pollination, which showed a knowledge of plant hybridisation. In 1838 Diebl and Napp had announced a prize to be awarded by the Pomological Association for the production of new varieties of currant bush. The first and second prizes were won by horticulturists, M. Frey and J. Tvrdý. In brief reports published in 1839 they described the methods of artificial pollination, including that later used by Mendel in his experiments. In 1846, with Napp's approval, Mendel attended Diebl's lectures on agriculture and pomology, and passed three examinations in these subjects.

Interest in science was given a new impetus in the province in the revolutionary year 1848, which saw the end of the long era of feudalism under the Habsburg Monarchy, although the convoked constitutional Parliament was broken up early in 1849 and an autocratic government came to power. However, a Provincial Assembly had been established, in which the adroit Abbot Napp held a leading position. He was also elected acting president of the Agricultural Society, which underwent further reorganisation in 1849–50. New specialised sections were formed. The Natural Science Section, the Pomicultural and Horticultural Section and the Apicultural Section all played an important part in Mendel's later activities.

The Natural Science Section started in November 1849, with twenty-seven members. By 1860 it already had 148, most of them teachers, doctors and pharmacists, and the remainder amateurs. According to the constitution, members were to investigate botany, zoology, mineralogy and geology in Moravia and Silesia, and to ensure the practical application of new knowledge. From the start they were also involved in meteorology, and soon to benefit from the co-operation of Mendel in that field. The chairman of the Natural Science Section was Count Mittrowsky, a liberal and a true friend of science.

Its leading light from 1854 was Alexander Zawadski (1798–1868), previously Professor of Mathematics and Physics at the University of Lemberg (now Lvov), and well known for his publications on botany, zoology, entomology, palaeontology and meteorology. As Dean of the Philosophy Faculty there he had been held responsible for student unrest, and had to resign his chair. In Brno he took up the post of teacher of physics and natural history at the newly established Realschule. (The Realschule—at sixth-form level, Oberrealschule— offered a 'vocational', or practical, education, as opposed to the classically orientated Gymnasium.) The director of the school was J. Auspitz (1812–88), who until 1848 had been a lecturer in mathematics and accounting at Vienna Technical College. But in that historic year he had, as a leader of the revolutionary guards, been forced to leave Vienna.

In 1854 Professor Zawadski published in the yearbook of the Realschule an article entitled 'The Demands of Present-Day Natural Scientific Investigation'. He tried to arouse interest in exact research and stressed the importance of searching for laws in the development of nature. Zawadski gave examples of scientists who had 'made the dark hours of the world's evolution brighter', and exhorted his pupils not to neglect natural history, which, he said, together with mathematics and chemistry, formed the basis of a realistic education, and which after Linnaeus he called 'the amiable science'. This idea of realistic education met with a positive response among pupils at the school and the members of the Natural Science Section were thus encouraged to cultivate pure science. One of these members was Gregor Mendel, who took up a post at the Realschule as a teacher of physics and natural history in the same year as Zawadski.

A landmark in the history of natural science in Brno came in 1859, when Bach's absolutist government in Vienna resigned. In the more favourable political climate which ensued, the natural scientists rebelled against the subordination of their section to the central committee of the Agricultural Society, dominated as it was by representatives of the erstwhile feudal landlords. After two years of negotiations an independent Natural Science Society was founded, in December 1861. Count Mittrowsky again became its chairman, with Professor Zawadski as his deputy. Mendel was among the enthusiastic founder-members. In 1862 its membership numbered 171. It also named twenty-four honorary members, who were mostly leading natural scientists and included

A. Braun, F. Unger, F. Wöhler, R. A. Bunsen and J. E. Purkyně.

The opening address at the constituent meeting of the Natural Science Society, held in the Realschule building, was given by Auspitz, who expressed his joy at the society's successful formation despite all difficulties. Its foundation, he declared, was motivated by deep interest in the cultivation of pure science.

At the second meeting, in 1862, the question of plant hybridisation was raised, and members subsequently referred to it more frequently. The problem of plant breeding and heredity had, of course, come up in discussion among plant breeders in Brno long before this, but within the framework of the new society the question began to be approached from a theoretical point of view.

OPAVA
FULNEK
HYNCICE
LIPNIK

OLOMOUC

BRNO

ZNOJMO

PRAGUE

BOHEMIA

CZECHO

SLOVAKIA

BRATISLAVA

VIENNA

Czechoslovakia

2   A gifted young man in search of an education

Gregor Mendel grew up among Moravians who, influenced by the Enlightenment and the French Revolution, believed in an ideal of progress distilled from a blend of philosophy and advances in science. Its effects could be felt even in the village school of Mendel's native Hynčice (Heinzendorf), a hamlet in northern Moravia.

His father, Anton Mendel (1789–1857), was a peasant, still bound by the old feudal law of corvée to work three days a week for his landlord; but eight years' military service in the Napoleonic Wars had brought him experience of ways of life and of farming methods in different parts of the Habsburg Monarchy. He was clearly both industrious and enterprising. On his return from the wars he built in Hynčice a new stone cottage, something unusual at that time and place. His wife Rosine, *née* Schwirtlich (1794–1862), came from a gardener's family in a neighbouring village. Her uncle, Anton Schwirtlich, who was self-educated, had taught in the small Hynčice schoolhouse at the end of the eighteenth century.

On 22 July 1822 Rosine Mendel gave birth to the family's only son, christened Johann (he assumed the name Gregor on his admission to the novitiate in 1843). Rosine had already given birth to three daughters, but the first two had died. The third, Veronika, was born in 1820, and a fourth daughter, Theresia, in 1829.

Most of the villagers of Hynčice, which lay on the ethnic watershed, thought of themselves as Germans (although some of Johann's forebears were from the nearby Czech village of Veselí, and it has been estimated that perhaps a quarter of his ancestors were Czechs). Mendel considered himself German and he published in German; but while in Brno he also read and spoke Czech and could, with some difficulty, write it. He counted among his friends a number of leading Czech figures.

The peasant's young son learned the rudiments of natural history well enough. Here, in the domain of an enlightened noblewoman, Countess Truchsess-Zeil, schoolmasters had instructions to teach the subject, with a view to improving the quality of village life and agricultural work. It was with this aim that the parish priest, Fr. J. Schreiber (1769–1850) had previously pioneered the teaching of natural history (and published a textbook) at the educational institute in nearby Kunín. This institute, which was modelled on one in Saxony where Christian Carl André once taught, was accused by the Jesuits after the French Revolution of 'introducing foreign Lutheran ideas'; and after several investigations it was finally closed. In the meantime Fr. Schreiber had been accused of 'aggravating the scandal' and in 1802 deprived of his position as teacher. He then turned up as priest in Dolní Vražné, a parish which included the hamlet where Mendel was born, and taught at the village school there.

While at Kunín, Schreiber had encouraged the cultivation of new fruit-tree varieties. It had been his idea for the countess to obtain grafts from France, and he saw to it that they were distributed among the villagers. Now, as parish priest, Schreiber established a fruit-tree nursery in the presbytery garden, and taught his parishioners how to cultivate and graft different varieties. Among those who obtained grafts from him was Mendel's father. Thus Schreiber combined his spiritual mission with that of educating his flock in the ways of nature, in the spirit of the Enlightenment. His efforts achieved recognition when the Brno Agricultural Society made him a corresponding member—no mean honour.

It was Schreiber who suggested that the Mendels send their gifted child to the Piarist school at Lipník, some twenty kilometres away, to see how he got on—the Piarists being an order renowned for their teaching skills. When the boy's talents were confirmed, his parents enrolled him in the Gymnasium in Opava, at a distance of fifty kilometres. The teachers there were also active naturalists, helping to build up natural history collections in the recently established museum. They also made very competent meteorological observations.

Johann's parents could offer him only limited financial support for his studies in the distant town, and he had to earn part of his keep. The family farm suffered the effects of repeated bad harvests and, to make matters worse, in 1838 Anton Mendel was injured while working in his landlord's forests, and had to give up farm work. The young man's position became precarious. He was later to record in his *curriculum vitae* (written in the third person) that, four years after entering the school, 'owing to successive disasters, his parents were quite unable to meet the expenses necessary to continue his studies, and it therefore happened that the respectfully undersigned, then only sixteen years old, was in the unfortunate position of having to provide for himself entirely.'

After finishing at Opava, Mendel evinced a strong desire to complete his education. His main concern was 'to secure for himself the necessary means for the continuation of his studies'. In the autumn of 1840 he enrolled for a two-year course at the Philosophy Institute attached to Olomouc University. This was necessary if he was to go on to study at university.

In Olomouc Mendel got into even direr straits than at Opava, not having the necessary connections to obtain references as a private tutor. Later he was to write: 'The distress occasioned by these disappointed hopes, and the anxious, dreary outlook which the future offered him, affected him so powerfully at that time that he fell sick, and was compelled to spend a year with his parents to recover.' Apparently through the intercession of his mother, Mendel's younger sister renounced part of her dowry to finance his studies, enabling him to repeat the first year and eventually finish his course. He remained duly grateful to her for the rest of his life.

The syllabus of the Philosophy Institute was centred on the study of theology, philosophy, mathematics and physics. A subsidiary subject was agricultural studies. Professors from the university taught at the institute, among them J. Fux, author of a mathematics textbook which stated basic principles that were to be important later in Mendel's explanation of his experiment results.

Mendel was at the end of his strength by the time he finished the course, feeling, as he put it, that 'it was impossible for him to endure such exertions any further'. But at this juncture Professor Franz, who taught physics and had previously lived in the Augustinian monastery at Brno, extended a helping hand. Through his connection with Abbot Napp he recommended Mendel be admitted to the Brno monastery, to allow him to continue his natural science studies. In his letter to

Napp, Franz spoke of the young man's academic success, stating that he was an excellent student of physics.

At the age of twenty-one Mendel was faced with the decision of a lifetime. At this crossroads in his career, as he was later to record, he 'felt himself compelled to enter a station in life which would free him from the bitter struggle for existence'. Taking up Franz's offer, he entered the novitiate in the Brno monastery in September 1843.

There are no documents explaining in detail Mendel's decision to enter the monastery. We only know that in 1838 when his father was injured and was unable to carry on working, his only son—who would traditionally have succeeded to the holding—refused to return home and run the farm. It was handed over to Alois Sturm, husband of Mendel's older sister Veronika. In the contract relating to its transfer was the provision that in the case of Johann's entering the priesthood, he was to receive some money, and the expenses connected with the first mass should be covered by Sturm. One can easily imagine that the young Mendel, influenced as he was by Fr. Schreiber, would think the position of an educated village priest attractive: he could devote himself to the natural sciences for the benefit of his parishioners. Entering the Augustinian monastery in Brno was Mendel's only chance of realising his intellectual ambitions.

Mendel soon found that he had moved into a cultural milieu which was exceptionally conducive to further studies. As he said in his *curriculum vitae* of 1850, this step brought a radical change in his circumstances. First he worked at the subjects laid down for the novitiate, but at the same time devoted every spare moment to private study of the natural sciences.

Just as Mendel was setting out his momentous course

of experiments, Abbot Napp was obliged to justify the monastery's scientific efforts in the face of bitter criticism from the Bishop of Brno, Schaffgotsche. The Church authorities, as part of the Catholic restoration then under way, were campaigning to tighten up the conditions of monastic life, and to this end Schaffgotsche was inspecting the monasteries of the Augustinian order. Abbot Napp prepared a report which pointed to the extraordinary privilege according to the terms of which the monastery was placed under the direct supervision of the order's superiors in Rome, and to an imperial decree of 1802, entrusting the monastery with the task of providing for the teaching of Bible studies, philosophy and mathematics at the newly established Philosophical Institute in Brno.

After a two-day visitation, the bishop came to the conclusion that Napp was so occupied with his public functions that he was neglecting his duties as abbot. The community, Schaffgotsche asserted, was devoting so much effort to its scientific activities that the interior, spiritual life of the order had been 'quite extinguished'. He insisted they revert to observance of the medieval *regula* of the mendicant monks, a suggestion which the abbot and his friars decisively rejected. The bishop demanded radical changes in the monks' way of life. He even suggested that the abbot be pensioned off to devote himself to public offices; that the monastery be abolished by extraordinary decree of the Papal See, and another, better disciplined order be summoned to Brno. The fate of individual monks was to be decided subsequently.

Napp took a firm stand against the conclusions reached in the wake of the bishop's visitation, and in a memorandum stressed the order's special privileges and described the excellent work the friars had done in the field of teaching. Of Mendel, Napp wrote that he was devoted to natural science and physics and was active as supply teacher of natural science in the Realschule; that currently he was at the monastery's expense at the Physics Institute in Vienna, to further his education in preparation for public teaching.

Mendel's fellow monks included philosophers and mathematicians, mineralogists and botanists. One of them, Fr. Aurelius Thaler (1796–1843), a mathematics teacher, was recognised in Brno as a pioneer in botany. In 1830 he set up an experimental plot beneath the refectory windows, growing rare plant species there. When Mendel entered the community in 1843, Thaler had died and responsibility for the experimental garden was taken over by Fr. Matthaeus Klácel (1808–82). Klácel was a botanist, with an interest in mineralogy and astronomy, and was already regarded as an expert in natural sciences. He became a member of the Prague Natural Science Society, and later of the Brno Agricultural Society. Klácel had other interests too. Both he and a fellow-monk, Thomas Bratránek, were philosophers, respected in the field and in contact with others. But in 1844, shortly after Mendel was admitted to the monastery, and despite Napp's efforts to defend him, Klácel was deprived of his post as a philosophy teacher, on the grounds that he was spreading pantheistic notions. In the revolutionary year 1848 he saw new hope for himself. At his instigation six members of the community, among them Mendel, sent the recently elected imperial assembly a petition 'in the name of humanity', asking for civil rights to be extended to monastic orders. They combined political demands with an attempt to win the right to devote themselves entirely to science and education. At the time Klácel was forty, and the oldest of the signatories. He expected to get the post of Professor of Philosophy in Prague. But in the ensuing period of repression he could no longer hope to teach and was only able to act as the monastery librarian.

When Mendel entered the monastery, Klácel, an older and more experienced botanist who was also engaged in crossing plants, became his mentor. In 1868, when Mendel was elected abbot, Klácel decided to go to the United States. He left the Church and worked as a journalist, pursuing Utopian social ideas and finally assuming a position of idealistic atheism. Though never able to understand Mendel's research, Klácel recalled from the United States his collaborator Gregor, his 'faithful companion' in natural science studies.

The climate of thought in the monastery had a great influence on Mendel as a natural scientist. As he said himself, his interest in the subject grew, and he was determined to miss no opportunity to extend his knowledge. While still studying theology, he welcomed the chance to attend Professor Diebl's lectures on natural history and agricultural science.

When his theological studies came to an end, Mendel spent a short time as chaplain at the nearby hospital. But daily exposure to the sufferings of the sick and dying so affected the compassionate young friar that he nearly became ill himself. Napp was sympathetic, and sent him in 1849 to teach at the Gymnasium in Znojmo. This was a watershed in Mendel's life. He taught mathematics and classics and was liked by the other staff for his modesty, expertise and competent teaching. The head of the school sent him to take his teacher's examination at Vienna University, which was at the time possible without previous study there. So Mendel took the examination in natural history for all Gymnasium grades, and in physics for the lower grades. Before the actual examination he had to submit two written works, on meteorological and geological topics. On the strength of these he took a written examination in physics and zoology. In both cases his knowledge of physics was regarded as sufficient, but he failed the examination because of his weakness in zoology.

Mendel returned to Brno with his desire for further education undiminished. As his knowledge of natural sciences was already recognised there, despite his failure in the teachers' examination the head of the Technical College asked him in the spring of 1851 to take over the natural history teaching during the professor's illness. At the end of three months' teaching there he was congratulated on his energy, competence and considerateness to his pupils.

In October of that year Abbot Napp wrote to the Bishop's Office that Fr. Mendel was unable to perform the duties of a parish priest, and that he had shown evidence of exceptional intellectual capacity, and remarkable industry, in the pursuit of natural sciences. Napp therefore recommended that he be sent to Vienna University. Mendel went there in October 1851, to study physics.

3 The university student and the problem of heredity

The research interests which led Mendel to his discovery grew out of a broad theoretical knowledge. It was at Vienna University, between 1851 and 1853, that he acquired the empirical, methodological and scientific skills which, in their interaction, made possible his later exact research on plants.

Abbot Napp sent Mendel to Vienna to study physics at the Institute of Professor Christian Doppler (1801–53), who gave his name to the Doppler effect, known to every physics student. Most biographies have omitted to point out that Mendel had no prescribed course, but was able to choose the subjects which most interested him. The other subjects Mendel selected were mathematics, chemistry, entomology, palaeontology, botany and plant physiology. The total number of hours for which he enrolled in physics, mathematics and chemistry made up about 70 per cent of the whole.

Additionally, Mendel attended a special course organised by Doppler for a maximum of twelve students on how to perform demonstrations in experimental physics. This was undoubtedly valuable for him. The headmaster of the Realschule in Brno, who annually endorsed Mendel's appointment as supply teacher, stressed that he was a good experimentalist and gave excellent demonstrations in physics and in natural history. Mendel considered himself above all an experimental physicist, as his correspondence shows.

A question often raised in connection with Mendel's research is the extent to which his university studies influenced the formation of his experimental programme and the crystallisation of his theory. Simplistic attempts have been made to find him precursors in research into plant hybridisation, but an understanding of Mendel's original methodological approach is not possible unless we take into account the whole of his programme of study. We then see that he assimilated all the basic scientific knowledge which made up the contemporary scientist's view of the world.

The predominant element in this view was the physical one, physics being at the time the most developed of the natural sciences. It taught that all nature was subject to laws, and that even the most complex phenomena could be explained by means of a small number of laws based on the existence of the smallest particles of matter. The goal of science was to learn about these particles, find the mathematical laws which governed their behaviour, and thus form a theory. Such laws could not be arrived at by random speculation, but must be based on planned experiments and be mathematically tested and proved.

In his research Mendel applied the methods of a physicist; but at the same time he made full use of empirical findings in plant hybridisation and the latest experiments with plant fertilisation. A comparison of his record of study in Vienna with those of his contemporaries who were also to take an interest in plant hybridisation, such as Kerner von Marilaun (1831–98), a well-known Austrian botanist, shows that none studied such an impressive combination of subjects as Mendel did. He thus underwent the right sort of preparation for his future work. All the components needed for planning his research into heredity and creating the theory were present in his university studies.

29

Research methods

By the mid-nineteenth century naturalists had begun to believe that everything in nature could be explained scientifically. This idea had its origin in physics, the most developed of the sciences. All phenomena were governed by laws, concerning the smallest particles of matter and their movement; the laws of nature were written in the language of mathematics. It was the task of the scientists to reveal these laws and create theories, experimentally proved. Such was the understanding of nature Mendel found in a textbook of experimental physics written by A. Baumgartner and E. Ettingshausen, with both of whom he came in contact. Baumgartner had originally been Professor of Physics at the University of Olomouc, where he wrote the first edition of his textbook in 1823. Later he moved to Vienna. Mendel came across him on his first attempt at the university examination in 1850, when he favourably assessed Mendel's knowledge of physics and encouraged his going to Vienna to study natural sciences. Ettingshausen taught Mendel mathematics, and, after Doppler's death, also physics.

According to Baumgartner and Ettingshausen 'the preparation of suitably organised experiments is the surest means of learning the ways of nature in its many aspects, of finding the key to the laws, and of understanding the interrelation of phenomena.' It was just this idea of planned experiments that figured prominently in Mendel's work. He devised a programme of experiments for several years ahead, with peas as a model plant, using the results to test and demonstrate the validity of his theory.

The same physics textbook emphasised that the aim of research was to work from observed natural phenomena towards the highest laws, from which further, sub-ordinate laws could then be deduced. Hence the explanation of a particular phenomenon became a question merely of deriving knowledge from such laws. The smaller the number of laws established, the deeper the understanding of the essence of the phenomena investigated. By 'the highest laws' the authors meant those fundamental laws which could not be derived merely by means of induction, but only through experiments. In this process mathematics played a role of immeasurable significance, and could be used in all cases where quantitative evaluation was involved. The authors added 'Only when the highest laws have been established will the subordinate laws, preliminarily derived by induction, attain their true significance and full justification.' Just such an approach can be found in Mendel's experiments with crossing peas.

Halfway through the last century statistical concepts also were finding their way into natural science research. At the time of Mendel's studies in Vienna the subject was already included in physics and mathematics lectures. Doppler in his textbook on mathematics dedicated one chapter to combinatorial theory and basic principles of probability calculation. The Director of the Institute of Astronomy in Vienna, Littrow, published in 1833 a small volume entitled *Probability Calculation as Used in Scientific and Practical Life*, explaining the basis of the theory worked out by Laplace. In the introduction he stressed that all phenomena, even the most trivial, though seeming quite independent of the great laws of nature, must inevitably be the product of eternal laws like those which govern the movement of the sun and of other bodies in the sky. According to Littrow, it was our ignorance of the relation between these phenomena and the eternal laws of the universe which led us sometimes to explain their dependence on certain finite causes, and sometimes to put them down to pure chance, solely according to whether or not they fell into a pattern we could recognise. Littrow stated that the relationships of all phenomena in nature seem at first completely random; but the greater the number of those phenomena that is considered, the closer they approach to certain constant relationships.

Mendel was acquainted with Littrow's work and when, soon after returning from the university, he took over the task of compiling records of meteorological observations in Moravia, he applied statistical principles. At the same time he was carrying out experiments with peas, and he applied the same principles.

Mendel found the concept of discrete units both in physics and in chemistry. Ettingshausen in his textbook *The Initial Basis of Physics*, published in Vienna in 1853, called the smallest parts of matter material points, and treated them mathematically. In his study of chemistry Mendel would have learnt of the atomic concept of chemistry and the theory of radicals. According to the latter, organisms were composed of units analogous to elements in inorganic matter, but consisting of combinations of those elements on a higher level of organisation.

Of particular interest were the lectures on plant physiology by Professor Franz Unger (1800–70). Unger was engaged in the scientific controversy over plant fertilisation and had written on the topic of obtaining new horticultural varieties through artificial fertilisation. He emphasised methodology in botanical research, and made a great impression on students; it may be assumed that Mendel was among his admirers. Unger's scientific views were influenced by M. J. Schleiden, whose name is associated with the research leading up to the cell theory. In his life's work, *Basic Principles of Scientific Botany* (1842–3), Schleiden emphasised that in botanical research scientists should elaborate theories in the same way as physicists and chemists did. His book was subtitled 'Botany as an Inductive Science'. In it, Schleiden formulated methodological maxims for scientific botany, rejecting every hypothesis which did not seek to explain the processes within the plant as resulting from changes in cells. He regarded the formation of cells as the principle of life, attributing infinite variability to their changes. Though Schleiden's experimental research brought no new scientific knowledge of any consequence, he influenced many of his contemporaries. One of these was Unger, though he disagreed with Schleiden's view that cells were formed spontaneously in the 'cell liquid' in a process analogous to crystallisation. Schleiden regarded the structureless cytoblastoma from which cells arose as a vital substance, which contradicted the materialistic principles propounded by Unger. Mendel had a copy of Schleiden's *Basic Principles of Scientific Botany*, and from it acquired a picture of the new orientation in botanical research. It followed that in his own research he tried to bring the results of his hybridising experiments into line with the concept of the cell.

The enigma of generation and plant fertilisation

When Mendel arrived in Vienna, universities were just beginning to teach that the plant consists of cells and hence all the diverse organs of plants are made of cells. Improved microscopes were revealing the structure of plant and animal tissue; the concept of a fundamental unit in the structure of all living systems was becoming widespread. According to Unger, writing in 1851, 'it is in the cell, and nowhere else, that the concentration of the whole essence of the plant must be sought.' Basing his research on the concept of the cell, Mendel had at the same time to consider the then controversial question of generation and fertilisation, which was closely connected with the enigma of inheritance.

In the course of the eighteenth century scientists had propounded dozens of theories of generation, most of them based on the presumption that a preformed embryo existed in the sperm (or pollen grain), or in the ovum. Occasionally views were expressed, termed 'epigenetic', asserting that the germ or embryo develops anew in each generation. The idealistic German natural philosopher Blumenbach, at the end of the eighteenth century, had ascribed epigenetic development to the action of a creative force inherent in living organisms. Speculations on generation were reviewed in 1795 in a zoology textbook by Christian Carl André; he confronted the theory of a creative force in epigenesis with observed facts noted when crossing animals and plants, showing the involvement of both parents in the formation of the offspring. André concluded that a convincing procreation theory had yet to be found. In 1812 in Brno he introduced the new concept of 'artificial selection' as the theoretical basis of sheep breeding.

Fifteen years later, in 1829, his colleague Nestler used the term 'generation' in the title of his lectures on heredity, thus emphasising the connection between these phenomena. Yet, in the 1830s, the process of generation was just as much of a mystery as it had been at the turn of the century. Towards the end of that decade, wool began being imported to Europe from the colonies, and wool production in Moravia lost its economic importance. In the same period the leading sheep breeders in Moravia died; after 1840 interest was lost in explaining the theory of the selection process, and of heredity, in sheep.

Physiologists began to take a renewed interest in the subject of generation when the cell theory came on the scene. R. Leuckart, Professor of Zoology at Giessen, adopting concepts introduced by biochemists, published his view that in the process of generation the seed acted upon the ovum either by transferring matter according to the laws of chemical affinity, or by a process of fermentation. Leuckart inclined towards the second hypothesis. He supposed that the contact of the seed gave the molecules in the ovum a specific movement, on the basis of which the embryo developed. He attributed the phenomena of heredity to the various movements of molecules, thus bringing together the questions of generation and heredity, and implying the involvement of both parents in the formation of the embryo.

Professor R. Wagner of Göttingen, the editor of the series in which Leuckart's monograph appeared, was not satisfied with this explanation. He recommended that the problem of heredity should first be attacked experimentally—expecting that the results would lead to an explanation of the problem of generation too. Anticipating the execution of crossing experiments involving large numbers of animals with different characters, which would be evaluated in succeeding generations, Wagner suggested that the principles of statistics and mathematics should be applied. He ended by referring to the view of the eminent physiologist J. Purkyně (1787–1869) that the generation process involved a fusion of the matter of the germ cells of both parents. Finally, Wagner added that the same problem was under discussion with respect to plant fertilisation.

Schleiden in 1837 came to the conclusion that the embryo developed from the pollen tube itself after its penetration into the embryonal sac. This was in contradiction to the previous concept of Giovanni Battista Amici (1786–1863), the Italian astronomer and microscopist, who had first observed the growth of the pollen tube in 1823; Amici later postulated that the pollen tube merely stimulated the development of a preformed embryo in the embryonal sac.

In 1851 the German botanist W. Hofmeister showed that neither Amici nor Schleiden was right, but that both parents were involved in the fertilisation of plants. A scientific dispute flared up, brought to an end in 1856 by a publication on the fertilisation of higher plants by another German botanist, Radlkofer, who gave a convincing explanation of the involvement of both parents, noting beneath the title of his book that it was 'a contribution to resolving the conflict'. Mendel, who had at the time reached a critical point in elaborating his research project, must have been aware that the question of plant fertilisation required elucidation.

A major contribution was made to the solution of the problem in 1855 by a pupil of Purkyně, N. Pringsheim, who in his experiments with freshwater algae demonstrated that one single antherozoon (spermatozoon) sufficed to accomplish the fertilisation process. Mendel was at the time well placed to learn all about Pringsheim's research and the plant fertilisation controversy through his close friendship with J. Nave, who studied law in Vienna while Mendel was studying natural sciences. Nave chose a career in law to assure his income, but botany attracted him much more. Later, in Brno, he devoted all his leisure to research on algae. In 1858 he published an extensive paper in Brno, 'On the development and propagation of algae', summarising the latest research in this line. He also drew attention to Pringsheim's 'brilliant' discovery of sex in algae and mentioned Unger's own research into algae and the fertilisation process.

Mendel arrived at Vienna University after the Botanical Institute had been split into an institute for systematic botany, where Professor Fenzl lectured, and another for plant physiology, headed by Professor Unger. The fertilisation dispute was just coming to a head. Fenzl was a proponent of the view that the embryo develops only from the pollen cell, while Unger emphasised that both parents contribute to its origin. Mendel sided with Unger, and in his work used terms introduced by the latter. When Mendel took his teacher's examinations for the second time, in 1856, Unger was absent and Fenzl was the examiner. How that examination went remains a mystery, as do the reasons why the records of it were lost, whereas those of the 1850 examinations are preserved in their entirety. We know only that Mendel sat the examinations, and that he returned to Brno in a state of depression. It has recently been suggested that Fenzl might have taken issue with Mendel's explanation of the fertilisation process; this could have given rise to a clash, resulting in Mendel's withdrawal from the examination.

In the concluding remarks of his paper on *Pisum*, Mendel wrote that 'according to the opinion of famous physiologists, propagation in phanerogams [higher plants] is initiated by the union of one germinal and one pollen cell into a single cell, which is able to develop

37

into an independent organism through the incorporation of matter and the formation of new cells.' His theory fitted together beautifully with the latest research into plant fertilisation. He referred to the 'opinion of famous physiologists' without giving their names, which was peculiar, because when he described his precursors in plant hybridisation he did give the names of the most important among them. We can assume he had in mind primarily Unger, but also Pringsheim and perhaps Purkyně, who in 1850 moved from Wroclav to Prague. There he met Klácel, and in 1855 visited Brno as a guest of the Augustinian monastery. Later Purkyně made further visits to Brno and to the monastery. On the occasion of his first visit the greenhouse was already built, and Mendel was beginning his experiments with peas. There is no direct evidence of Purkyně's having spoken to Mendel, but it is highly probable that, seeing the experimental garden, he would have taken an interest in the experiments, and perhaps have expressed his views on fertilisation.

Thus we see that after 1850 other naturalists were interested in experimental plant hybridisation and in investigating the process of plant fertilisation. Mendel was acquainted with the relevant papers and was familiar with the controversy over generation and fertilisation.

Plant hybridisation and heredity

The German botanist C. F. Gärtner reviewed experimental research on hybridisation in an extensive monograph which appeared in 1849. Mendel owned a copy, and his marginalia and notes on the flyleaf suggest that he studied it in detail several times. He thus acquired an up-to-date picture of knowledge on plant hybridisation, and at the same time advice on further research into the question.

Gärtner described separately nearly all the phenomena that later occurred in the definitions of the so-called Mendelian Laws of Heredity, with the exception of the most important, those providing the theoretical basis for the numerical segregation ratios. On the inside of the back cover of Gärtner's book Mendel noted character pairs in peas, which he later studied as his model experimental plant. Among the points Gärtner made was that the elucidation of the origin and development of hybrids from the elements and characters of their parents is important both for plant physiology and for the classification of different plant forms. Gärtner also led Mendel to study a German translation of Seton and Goss's papers, published in England in 1824, which described experiments there with peas. These papers demonstrated dominance and the segregation of characters in the hybrid progeny (see below, pp. 45 ff.), but only implicitly. Mendel referred to Gärtner's book right at the outset of his paper, but he pointed out that 'no generally applicable law of the formation and development of hybrids has yet been successfully formulated'.

Mendel almost certainly heard about the problem of plant hybridisation in Unger's lectures. The latter published in 1851 his *Botanical Letters*, which drew attention to modern research trends in botany. He advocated a planned experimental study of the way in which plant characters developed, and recommended that observations be made over several successive generations. In agreement with the pioneers in physiological research, Unger supposed that both parents participated in the production of the embryo. He was also convinced that differences between individual plants were the result of particular arrangements of certain elements inside the cells, elements which he believed to have a physical existence. According to him such units could be derived from others, and undergo changes. He used this idea to explain the developmental process in nature. The appearance of new characters and even new species was, he thought, the result of a combination of elements inside the cell.

In his publications Unger often mentioned Carl Nägeli (1817–91), Professor of Botany at Munich. Very probably he also referred to him in his lectures, which might have been what led Mendel to send Nägeli reprints of his *Pisum* paper. The eminent botanist and the newcomer to research embarked on a prolonged correspondence, which lasted from 1867 to 1873.

Unger's work influenced research even some distance away. Hugo de Vries in Amsterdam, later to become famous as one of those who rediscovered Mendel's paper, quoted beneath the title of a dissertation published in 1870 Unger's statement that 'The task of physiology is to translate the phenomena of life into the known laws of physics and chemistry.' It was this new, reductionist trend which led Hugo de Vries in 1889 to his concept of a unit of heredity.

When Unger died, the secretary of the Natural Science Society in Brno, Niessl, spoke of how he had 'seen far beyond his study walls' and had been 'one of the leading intellects of our century'. Among the members of the society whom Unger inspired was Mendel, who, on his return from Vienna, immediately began to plan his experiments. His aim was to explain the law of the origin and development of hybrids. He was fully aware of the complexities of the task and of the other important problems involved, such as the perennial enigma of generation and evolution, which was closely connected with the mystery of heredity.

4 The *Pisum* experiments

Mendel originally wrote his account of the experiments with *Pisum* in the form of two lectures for meetings of the Natural Science Society, early in 1865. After the second of these the secretary of the society asked him to publish the text, which he then reread carefully and sent to the printer's unchanged, having found no 'source of error'. His lectures were designed to arouse his audience's interest both in his new method of experimenting with plant hybrids (a subject already discussed at earlier meetings), and in his theoretical explanation.

Mendel began by describing experiments that involved crossing and testing a large number of plants, the aim being to examine how their characters were passed on from generation to generation. His results presented a more accurate picture of the facts than those of his predecessors, and he was the first to generalise his findings in terms of mathematical symbols. The second lecture investigated the composition of hybrid cells from the broad physiological viewpoint, on the then new level of cell theory. It contains a bold explanation of the theoretical mechanism of inheritance, and it is here that the brilliance of Mendel's mind is revealed. As he forms and refines his theory, we can see his genius at work.

On both occasions Mendel adroitly interspersed his report on his observations with measured doses of theory. He did not give full details of his experiments, which he had planned using experience gained in previous ones that he did not even mention. This made for conciseness and clarity in his account, but at the same time has hindered attempts to reconstruct his experiments. Another obstacle to full comprehension of his theory is Mendel's terse exposition.

The motivation of Mendel's investigation, and its goal, are revealed in the opening sentences of his lecture:

> Artificial fertilisation undertaken on ornamental plants to obtain new colour variants initiated the experiments to be discussed here. The striking regularity with which the same hybrid forms always reappeared whenever fertilisation between like species took place suggested further experiments, whose object it was to follow the development of hybrids in their progeny.

The text of the first lecture goes on to describe the arrangement and sequence of experiments, but not without first emphasising that the selection of plants for such experiments demands the greatest possible care. Mendel's own rigorous attitude is indicated by his comments on the work of Gärtner, then considered the leading authority on the subject. In a copy of the latter's monograph on hybridising experiments Mendel marked a passage referring to somewhat similar work on hybrids of *Mirabilis* (four-o'clock). In a letter to Nägeli he noted that 'this worthy man' had 'not published a detailed description of his individual experiments' nor 'diagnosed his hybrid types sufficiently, especially those resulting from the same crossing'. Mendel dismissed Gärtner's findings as being too general and unclear for any definite conclusion to be drawn from them. His own experiments were designed to offer an explanation of what was observed.

Though Mendel was not the first to experiment with

the artificial fertilisation of plants, his precursors had for the most part confined their attention to the overall appearance of parents and offspring. As a result they subscribed to the age-old view that the characteristics of the parents 'blended' in the offspring. Charles Darwin was among those who thought in terms of this 'blending inheritance'.

Mendel reduced the problem to individual characters, choosing those which occurred in one of two variants. He then recorded and systematically analysed the pattern in which these alternative characters appeared in successive generations. After some preliminary experiments with several members of the family *Leguminosae*, he concluded that the plants of the genus *Pisum* were admirably suited to his purpose. They have some quite distinct characters in seeds and in plants that are easily and reliably distinguishable, and, moreover, they yield perfectly fertile hybrids. It is important to bear in mind that for Mendel the word hybrid refers only to the product of the first crossing—the F_1 generaton.

Over a two-year period Mendel studied thirty-four varieties of edible pea, differing in fifteen alternative characters. For his experiments he selected twenty-two which bred true, i.e. which did not vary over those years. These were distinguished by the following characters:

>seed shape: round or angular
>seed colour: yellow or green
>colour of the seed coat: white or grey-brown
>shape of the ripe pod: smoothly arched or deeply ridged between seeds
>colour of the unripe pod: light to dark green or bright yellow
>position of flowers: axillary or terminal
>length of stem: 1·9–2·2 m or 0·24–0·46 m.

Though Mendel's immediate precursors failed to test the constancy of the characters of their experimental plants, a similar two-year period of verification was mentioned in 1799 by Thomas Andrew Knight, who tried to find out what role each parent played in the production of offspring. Mendel may have learned the importance of this precaution from the lectures of Professor Diebl, in connection with breeding new plant varieties.

Another unique feature of Mendel's research programme was the scale on which he planned his experiments. He was convinced that the larger the number of separate measurements the more likely it was that a mere chance effect would be eliminated. He was thus a pioneer in applying statistics to biological research. His experiments with *Pisum* spanned the period 1854–63, and a reconstruction shows that they must have included some 28,000 plants, of which he 'carefully examined' 12,835. He used both an experimental plot, 35 m × 7 m, and the new greenhouse.

The key passage in the first part of Mendel's classic paper is that dealing with two experiments involving the shape and colour of seeds. They were also the experiments with which he dealt in greatest detail, noting that they 'lead most easily and surely to the goal'.

The first experiment was in essence very simple indeed, though, as we have seen, it had to be prepared with great care and was repeated many times over using all seven pairs of characters. Nor, clearly, were its implications easy to grasp, as history has proved.

An examination of the results Mendel obtained for one of his seven pairs will best illustrate the whole of his first experiment. He took plants from a pure-bred variety bearing round seeds and crossed them with a pure-bred variety with angular seeds. The resulting hybrid seeds

(F_1 generation) were all round; i.e. they acquired their shape from the round-seeded parent. The result was the same regardless of which parental variety provided the ovules and which the pollen. In the next season Mendel planted the round hybrid seeds, and, by self-fertilisation, obtained from them a generation of plants (F_2 generation) which yielded 5,474 round seeds and 1,850 angular ones. He recorded similar proportions of parental characters in the other six experiments, demonstrating that the characters segregate in the ratio 3:1.

The seeds of the hybrid generation (F_1) were not visibly distinguishable from those of the round-seeded parent. But in the F_2 generation, the angular shape reappeared. Mendel concluded that it had been present in some latent form in the hybrid, and without contamination by the round. Because the round shape had prevailed over the angular, Mendel called the former *dominant*, and the angular shape, which had receded, he denoted *recessive*. This was his first important finding. Plant characters did not blend in hybrids: they were transmitted as *discrete* factors. Mendel thus definitively rejected the notion of blending inheritance. This led him to continue his experiments in subsequent generations, which his precursors and contemporaries had never considered.

In the next season, Mendel planted both the round and the angular seeds produced by the F_2 generation, and the resulting plants, when self-fertilised, yielded the seeds of the next generation (F_3). An analysis of these seeds showed that those from the angular seeds were exclusively angular. But one-third of the round F_2 seeds produced exclusively round seeds, while the other two-thirds gave both round and angular seeds, again in the ratio 3:1. Mendel in fact investigated a further four generations to confirm his findings.

Here we will introduce a number of modern refinements, in particular, the terms now used to describe genetic phenomena. The factors which determine the hereditary transmission of characters are called *genes*, a term coined by Johannsen in 1909. In the Mendelian theory, an individual has two genes for each character. These two may be the same, or they may differ; usually there is more than one form in which they can occur. The different forms of a gene are called *alleles*. Depending on the gene, there may be one, two or some higher number of alleles in the whole population of organisms; but for the *Pisum* characters which Mendel chose there were only two alleles, producing plants with only two alternative forms of those characters.

Mendel's *Pisum* experiments revealed the existence of dominant alleles, such as that determining round seed shape, and recessive alleles, such as that determining angular seed shape. The former he denoted *A*, the latter *a*. His parent plants, which bred true, carried respectively only the *A* and the *a* alleles. The alleles carried are called the *genotype* of the trait. Organisms in which both alleles for a character are alike are called *homozygotes* with respect to that character, and they and their pure-bred offspring will always exhibit the character which that allele produces. The manifestation of the character is called the *phenotype*. The fact that it may be produced by different genotypes is the key to the whole enigma of hybridism.

Mendel deduced that his hybrid plants acquired one factor (gene) from each parent. Plants, like other sexual organisms, reproduce through *gametes*—pollen from the male, ovules from the female. In reproduction, the

47

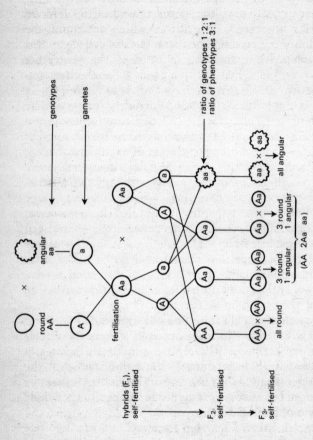

Fig. 1. Mendelian cross of two different true-breeding parental lines, *round* and *angular*. The hybrids are all round, but when crossed together do not breed true. Round and angular peas segregate in the ratio 3:1.

parent's double complement of genes is halved, and each gamete contains only a single factor. The hybrids were produced in Mendel's experiment when the *A*-bearing gametes from one parent joined the *a*-bearing gametes from the other: they were all *Aa* and, as we should now say, *heterozygotes*. These hybrids were all round, for this was where dominance came in. In the heterozygote genotype *Aa*, the allele *A* for round seed shape was dominant, and so this genotype produced the same phenotype as the genotype *AA*. When the hybrids were self-fertilised, equal numbers of the factors *A* and *a* combined at random to give plants with the seed genotypes *AA*, *Aa* and *aa* in the ratio 1:2:1. Because round shape is dominant to angular, *AA* and *Aa* are both round; and therefore the round and angular seed phenotypes occurred in the ratio 3:1. On average, of every three plants from the round seeds, one, with the *AA* genotype, again produced round and angular seeds in the ratio 3:1. The simple method of using letter symbols to denote dominant and recessive characters was adopted after 1900 for planning and analysing genetic experiments. Mendel's findings are illustrated, using this notation, in Fig. 1.

In generalising these results Mendel was able to put to good use what he had learned at Vienna University when studying combinatorial mathematics and probability theory. The way alleles combine according to the laws of probability in the most simple experiment is illustrated in the form of a checkerboard in Fig. 2.

For one pair of differing characters Mendel gave the resulting mathematical expression

$$AA + 2\,Aa + aa$$

which denoted the simple series in the progeny of

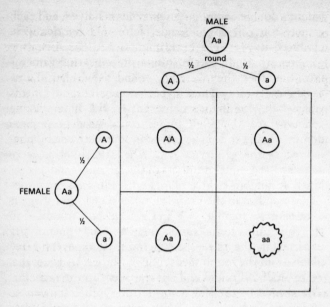

Fig. 2. Cross of two hybrid round peas, showing probabilities of producing different kinds of progeny. The parents both have genotype *Aa*. The male parent produces pollen in the ratio ½*A*:½*a*; the female parent produces ovules in the ratio ½*A*:½*a*. Combined at random, they produce ¼*AA*:½*Aa*:¼*aa*. The *AA* and *Aa* are both round, which gives a ratio of 3 round:1 angular.

hybrids (in his paper Mendel actually simplified this series to $A + 2Aa + a$). The expression implies both the segregation ratios, of 3:1 for the phenotypes and 1:2:1 for the genotypes (*AA*, *Aa* and *aa*), which are illustrated in Fig. 1.

In his next experiment Mendel investigated whether the law deduced for peas differing in one character only would hold good in the case where plants differed in two or more characters. He crossed pure-bred pea varieties whose seeds differed in both shape and colour, denoting the different alternative characters *A*, *a*, *B*, *b*. Growing peas from these hybrid seeds, Mendel obtained plants with a total of 556 seeds, comprising not only both parental types but also combinations of them. Some pods even contained all four kinds of seeds. The phenotypes obtained were as follows:

> 315 round and yellow
> 101 angular and yellow
> 108 round and green
> 32 angular and green

These results are illustrated in Fig. 3.

Mendel was not surprised to find that the hybrid (F₁) seeds were all round and yellow, for he had already observed a similar situation in the previous experiments with a single pair of characters. The Figure shows the sixteen combinations of alleles which occur in the progeny of hybrids. Nine of them are differently constituted, i.e. represent different genotypes. Of these the forms *AABB* and *aabb* are identical to the parental types, and the forms *AAbb* and *aaBB* are homozygotes combining the parental characters. These are the four combinations occurring in the diagonal top-left–bottom-right. They represent the four different phenotypes in the hybrid progeny, to which all the other combinations belong. Of the sixteen combinations, nine give round and yellow seeds, three give round and green seeds, three give angular and yellow seeds, and one gives angular and green seeds. This is the theoretical ratio of 9:3:3:1 which was borne out in Mendel's results. He expressed it as a combination of two simple series:

Mendel

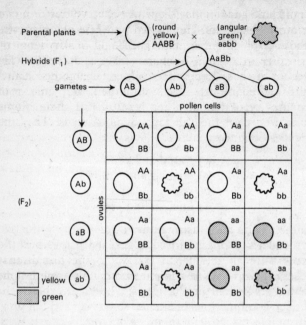

Fig. 3. Results of a dihybrid cross (i.e. between two varieties of pea differing in two independent characters), showing actual numerical ratios of the progeny: 9 round yellow, 3 angular yellow, 3 round green, 1 angular green.

$$AA + 2\,Aa + aa$$
$$BB + 2\,Bb + bb$$

producing the combination series
$AABB + AAbb + aaBB + aabb + 2\,AABb + 2\,aaBb + 2\,AaBB + 2\,Aabb + 4\,AaBb$.

In a similar manner Mendel demonstrated the combination of simple series for three pairs of characters: round and angular shape of seeds, yellow or green colour of seeds and grey-brown or white colour of the seed coat. He said that, not surprisingly, of all his experiments this demanded the most time and effort. He reached the conclusion that 'constant characters occurring in different forms of a plant kindred can, by means of repeated fertilisation, enter into all the associations possible within the rules of combination.' Finally, he added that he had actually obtained all the constant associations theoretically possible in *Pisum* through a combination of all seven characters which he studied, and that there were 128 of them, or 2^7.

Mendel's ideal was to present his theory in terms of mathematics, like a physicist. 'If n', he wrote, 'designates the number of characteristic differences in the two parental plants, then 3^n is the number of terms in the combination series, 4^n the number of individuals that belong to the series, and 2^n the number of combinations that remain constant.' According to the experiment shown in Fig. 3 this would mean 4^2 ways of arriving at 3^2 effective genotypes, giving in turn 2^2 phenotypes. Mendel's mathematical expressions, now incorporated into teaching on genetics, established the manner of planning genetical experiments and predicting the appearance of new combinations of characters. His explanation of the random combination of any number of characters came to be known as Mendel's Law of Independent Assortment.

In his second lecture Mendel described the results of experiments involving a relatively small number of plants. These were designed 'to throw light on the composition of seed and pollen cells in hybrids'. He discussed the results of the previous experiments with plants differing in one, two and three pairs of characters in relation to the then controversial questions of how plants were fertilised and how the embryo came into existence. Here he transposed his explanation to the plane of cell theory, which was just starting to make its mark in biological research. As has been outlined in the previous chapter, discussion on this topic reached a climax around the period when Mendel was studying in Vienna and starting his experiments. In 1855, it had been shown in algae that both parent forms are involved in the production of an embryo. By the time Mendel had concluded his experiments, this explanation had been extended to the higher plants, though it was still uncertain whether one or more pollen grains were required to fertilise the egg. In forming his theory Mendel adopted a remarkably accurate hypothesis regarding this question, which was a prerequisite for his conception of the transmission of hereditary characters.

First Mendel described experiments where he artificially fertilised *AaBb* hybrid plants using the pollen of plants carrying the dominant characters *AABB* and the recessive characters *aabb* respectively. Conversely, he fertilised both these homozygote forms with the pollen of the hybrid plant. The results of this test of the composition of hybrid cells are shown in Fig. 4:1.

In accordance with his theoretical expectation, Mendel demonstrated that a cross between the hybrid form and the dominant homozygote yielded only plants with the dominant characters, without segregation of the recessive ones. But when he crossed the hybrid with the

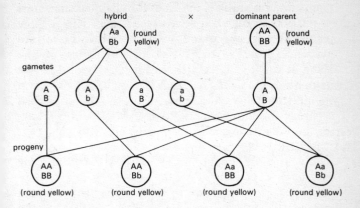

Fig. 4.1. Backcross of hybrid with dominant parent.

When the hybrids (e.g. round yellow) are crossed with their parental strains (which is called a backcross), the ratios of progeny types depend on which parental strain is used. In a cross with the dominant parental strain, all the progeny are identical.

recessive homozygote he produced the segregation of all the characters contained in the hybrid genotype, in the ratio 1:1:1:1. He confirmed these results in a further, particularly perspicacious experiment, where he crossed plants which were recessive monozygotes in one character, and heterozygotes in the other, the two parent plants having the opposite genotypes (see Fig. 4.2). The results again showed a segregation of characters in the ratio 1:1:1:1.

Mendel believed that these experiments reinforced and extended what he had proved in the experiments

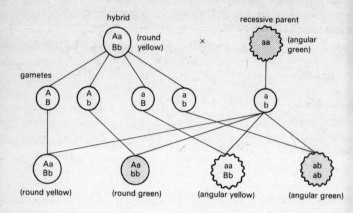

Fig. 4.2. Backcross of hybrid with recessive parent.

In a backcross with the recessive parental strain, the four different types of progeny segregate out in equal proportions

that dealt with pairs of characters. This section, 'The Reproductive Cells of Hybrids', concludes:

> The law of combination of different characters which governs the development of the hybrids therefore has its foundation and explanation in the principle enunciated, that the hybrids produce ovules and pollen cells which in equal numbers represent all constant forms which result from the combination of the characters brought together in fertilisation.

We get a clearer idea of what he meant by this in the final section of the lecture, where Mendel returns to the implications of his results for the physiology of plant fertilisation. Invoking the views of 'famous physiologists' (whom he did not name), he explained that 'for the purpose of propagation one pollen cell and one ovule unite in phanerogams into a single cell, which is capable by the assimilation and formation of new cells of becoming an independent organism.' In effect Mendel was giving a physicist's (indirect) proof that one pollen grain fertilises the egg. This was proved observationally under the microscope twenty years later. Mendel's footnote speaks for itself: 'How else could one explain that both parental types recur in equal numbers and with all their characteristics in the offspring of hybrids?'

Having thus disposed of the question of the fertilisation process, Mendel went on to explain how the experimental data allowed one to form a picture of the determinants which transferred characters from generation to generation. These he denoted 'potentially formative elements'. We should now say they were the units of heredity, the genes. Mendel was unable to describe the physical mechanism, but merely said: 'This development follows a constant law, which is based on the material composition and arrangement of the elements meeting in the cell in a viable union.' He thus formulated the fundamental theory of heredity, which was later shown to be completely correct and of universal applicability.

Publications concerning Mendel's research have often underestimated the second part of his paper, dealing with the reproductive cells of hybrids. Mendel himself considered the experiments to constitute very convincing support for his theory, and in his lecture stressed the importance of repeating these in particular. Later, in a letter to Nägeli, he suggested the latter should conduct similar crossing experiments using plants with

57

genotypes *AABb*, *AaBB* and *AaBb* and the pollen of plants which were *aabb*. He even supplied him with the necessary seeds, but Nägeli declined to make use of this opportunity to verify Mendel's conclusions.

It has not always been borne in mind that Mendel's lectures were well received by Brno naturalists. The journal *Neuigkeiten* reported that Mendel had given a 'long lecture, apparently of great interest to botanists, on plant hybrids obtained through the artificial pollination of related species by transferring the male flower pollen to the seed plants'. Mendel, the journal added, had shown that 'the hybrids are fertile, but not constant, having a tendency to revert in the progeny to the parental forms; this reversion may be accelerated by repeated artificial fertilisation with the pollen of the original plant forms.' In conclusion it was further stressed that there were 'remarkable' numerical ratios of characters occurring in hybrids. The report states that the lecture was very well attended and the lively participation of the audience showed that 'the choice of theme for the lecture was a happy one, and its delivery satisfactory.' The same journal also published a report on the second lecture in March, saying that Mendel had spoken on the formation of cells, fertilisation, and the formation of seeds in general, and especially in hybrids. It was emphasised that he had carried out his experiments with the greatest care, and had also mentioned experiments with other plant species. On the basis of favourable results obtained he felt encouraged not only to continue his hybridising experiments, but also to report on them again.

Both the meetings where Mendel delivered his lectures were chaired by C. Theimer, who had already spoken in 1862 on the occurrence of hybrid plants in nature. At the

end of Mendel's second lecture, the secretary of the
Natural Science Society, Niessl, a geodesist at the Technical College who was also interested in botany, added
that he had himself observed hybridisation in fungi,
mosses and algae with the help of a microscope, and that
'further studies in this field may not only justify the
existing hypothesis, but also provide an interesting
explanation.'

There was definite interest in Mendel's 1865 Brno
lectures. But the fact remains that no participant saw the
far-reaching implications of his theory, and no one tried
to repeat the experiments or to carry out similar experiments with other plant species. It may be assumed this
was because no other naturalist in Brno had such a
garden and greenhouse at his disposal, or the free time to
perform experiments on so large a scale.

Experiments with other plant species

The *Pisum* paper itself briefly mentions Mendel's
experiments with *Phaseolus* (bean), in which he set out
to discover whether the law of development found for
Pisum also applied to hybrids of other plants. He crossed
bean varieties with differences in the height of the plant,
the shape of the ripe pods, and the colour of both blossoms and unripe pods. In respect to the first two characters, despite a degree of infertility which limited the
number of plants obtained, Mendel was able to conclude
that 'the development of hybrids follows the same law as
in *Pisum*.' In the case of the colour characters, however,
a more complex picture emerged. The hybrid between
beans with white and crimson blossoms respectively
had flowers which were less intensely crimson than its
parent, and though the white colour reappeared
unchanged in the hybrid progeny, the remainder of the

plants had flowers varying from crimson to pale violet. The unripe seed pods exhibited a similar range of variation in colouring.

Mendel, far from being discouraged by this complication, once more demonstrated his ability to create a hypothesis. This phenomenon, too, he wrote, can be explained by means of the law valid for *Pisum*, 'if one might assume that the colour of flowers and seeds is composed of two or more independent colours that behave individually like any other constant characters in the plant'. He was quite right. Sticking to his original idea, he made the necessary modifications to his notation, and proceeded to explain the complex coloration on the same basis of mathematical series. The dominant crimson colour, he proposed, might be composed of the two colour elements A_1 and A_2, which by appearing together produced crimson. The hybrids resulting from the crossing with the recessive white colour would acquire the genotype $A_1a + A_2a$ and when propagated would give the series

$$A_1 + 2A_1a + a$$
$$A_2 + 2A_2a + a \quad\underline{\hspace{1.5cm}}$$

—different combinations of whose terms would be responsible for the various colours.

Mendel's scientific integrity obliged him to admit that this explanation rested 'on a mere supposition', because of the very scant material on which it was based. He recommended once again that similar experiments on flower coloration be performed, since it was probable that 'through this approach we may learn to understand the extraordinary diversity of coloration in our ornamental plants'.

He also offered a general theoretical assessment of the

possibility that the environment affected the variability of plant characters. Noting that the view had often been expressed that species stability was upset or even destroyed when plants were cultivated (coloration being a case in point), he stated decisively that 'no one would seriously want to maintain that plant development in the wild and in garden beds was governed by different laws.' His own experience suggested another explanation: 'Various experiments force us to accept the opinion that our cultivated plants, with few exceptions, are members of different hybrid series, whose development along regular lines is altered and retarded by frequent intraspecific crosses.' He had thus become convinced that the colour of garden plants was governed by a law 'which possibly finds expression through the combination of several independent colour characters'.

In the years following 1865 Mendel continued his experiments on a number of other plant species. The chief source of information on these is his letters to Nägeli, who had published a number of extensive articles on plant hybridisation from the taxonomical point of view, and who later, under the influence of Darwin, considered evolutionary aspects of the question. Nägeli was particularly interested in the hybridisation of hawkweed, which became the focus of his attention during the correspondence. He seems to have at first underestimated Mendel's investigation. Later, however, he revised his opinion and we may note that Mendel, addressing him, switched from his original formal salutation 'Highly Esteemed Sir' to 'Highly Esteemed Friend'. The change in attitude in the correspondence is most apparent in the closing words of Nägeli's letter of 27 April 1870: 'I consider myself indeed

fortunate to have found in you such a skilled and successful colleague.'

In his *Pisum* research Mendel had investigated the
progeny of hybrids known to exhibit segregation of characters, which he called variable hybrids. But he noted at
the time that there were exceptional hybrid forms, e.g.
Dianthus, which were described as constant, where hy-
bridisers mentioned no such segregation in the progeny.
In his second lecture he had stated that 'whether
variable hybrids of other plants species show complete
agreement in behaviour remains to be decided experimentally'. He experimented with a further fourteen
genera which confirmed his theory.

In 1869 Mendel concluded experiments with *Matthiola* (stock), *Zea* (maize) and *Mirabilis* (four-o'clock), and
stated in his eighth letter to Nägeli that their hybrids
had behaved exactly like *Pisum*.

In experiments with thirty-six varieties of *Matthiola*
he encountered more complex coloration of blossoms
than in beans, and, again by analogy with *Pisum*, wished
to attribute this to still more complicated composed
series. In the experiments with *Lychnis* (campion)—an
example of a plant with sexes—Mendel observed
another remarkable phenomenon. He saw in the hybrid
progeny segregation into sexes—male and female—and
tried to explain this, too, on the same basis as the
transmission of characters. It was only after the turn of
the century that the phenomenon of hereditary determi-
nation of sex in plants came to be understood.

Constant hybrid forms: the hawkweed experiments

If in his experiments with *Pisum* and other species Mendel had sought to explain the law of the origin and
development of hybrids, in his work on *Hieracium*

(hawkweed) he was seeking an explanation for a different phenomenon, that of the apparent constancy of some hybrid forms. The subject earned a brief mention at the end of the *Pisum* paper itself, but in 1865 Mendel was able to say no more about the nature of such hybrids than what had already been published on the subject. None the less, he did toy with a possible explanation, offering the tentative hypothesis that different elements might associate temporarily or permanently. But he added a cautionary note that 'this attempt to relate an important difference in the development of hybrids to a permanent or temporary association of differing cell elements can, of course, be of value only as a hypothesis which, for lack of well-substantiated data, still leaves some latitude.'

Towards the end of 1867 Mendel was impatiently awaiting the results of his experiments with *Hieracium*, *Geum* (herb-bennet) and *Linaria* (flax), which were intended to clear up the question of the existence of constant hybrids. He wrote that the progeny of the hybrid *Geum urbanum-rivulare*, said by Gärtner to be constant, 'varied somewhat in flower size'. Mendel no longer considered the published data convincing. In the end he resolved to concentrate in his further research on testing the constancy of hybrid forms, using hawkweed. Whereas with *Pisum* he had used different characters in the same species, with *Hieracium* he worked on the level of the genus, crossing plants of different species. The experiments were no less important to Mendel than those with *Pisum*. The technique of artificially pollinating the small flowers of hawkweed was extremely difficult, and Mendel hoped for some helpful suggestions from Nägeli. In fact the latter was unable to offer any advice, since he had not carried out experiments of the same kind. At first Mendel failed to obtain hybrids. When he finally did meet with success, Nägeli had high praise for him.

The profusion of transitional forms of *Hieracium* had attracted the interest of researchers. Some forms of the plant were considered to be interspecific hybrids, though this remained unproved. Mendel investigated the existence of hybrids in the genus from the taxonomical, evolutionary and ecological points of view. A detailed evaluation of individual plants at last showed one to be a hybrid. In 1867 Mendel was able to inform Nägeli of further hybrid plants. He soon realised that he was confronted here with a very complex problem of the physiology of fertilisation which required much more comprehensive research.

Mendel reported his findings at a meeting of the Natural Science Society in July 1869. Describing six hybrid forms, he noted the difficulties involved in artificially pollinating a genus with flowers so minute and of such peculiar shape. It was still necessary, Mendel asserted, to verify experimentally whether the rules found for other plant species also applied to *Hieracium*. He was obliged to admit that, in contrast to those of *Pisum*, the *Hieracium* hybrids he had obtained were not uniform, nor was their progeny variable; he even went so far as to say that 'In *Hieracium*, according to the present experiments, the exactly opposite phenomenon seems to be exhibited.' Still, he considered the mooted constancy of some hybrids 'an open question'. In the published text of the lecture Mendel confessed that he had some scruples about giving an account of experiments just begun; since, however, to carry out the proposed experiments would take many years, which he could not be sure

God would grant him, he had decided to pass on his preliminary results.

The *Hieracium* experiments were particularly exacting, but Mendel assiduously continued to develop his theory in the face of seemingly contradictory results. The hawkweed had to be pollinated with the aid of a magnifying glass and in artificial light; in June 1870 Mendel complained of failing eyesight, which forced him to discontinue his work. Later it became clear that in his new role as abbot he would not be able to perform the projected experiments. He expressed to Nägeli his disappointment at this turn of events.

The complicating factor which dogged the experiments with hawkweed was the rare phenomenon of asexual reproduction, later called apogamy. This exceptional form of plant reproduction, found in *Hieracium*, was something Mendel could not have anticipated; it was not explained until 1903. Mendel did in the end obtain true hybrids, and his perseverance and powers of observation led him to demonstrate the segregation of characters in their progeny. He concluded that each hybrid character appears in a certain number of variants which represent different transitional stages between one ancestral character and the other. 'It seems that the variants of the different characters may occur in all possible combinations.' In this conclusion Mendel indicated that the results with *Hieracium* conformed with the theory derived for *Pisum*. In this case, however, series even more complex than those suggested for *Phaseolus* and *Matthiola* had to be assumed. A surviving fragment of Mendel's notes shows that he supposed the series for *Hieracium* to be very complex indeed, and he therefore thought there was little hope of observing segregated characters in the minute blossoms of a small number of experimental plants.

Later in his research with hawkweed Mendel was intent on finding out why its hybrids exhibited low fertility. He quoted Gärtner's view that the pollen of the parent forms is 'more potent' than that of hybrids. This was intended to explain the impossibility of fertilising hybrid plants with their own pollen. Mendel in his research found that there were great differences in the capacity of flowers for fertilisation. Where hybrids were infertile, he assumed that their pollen was incapable of fertilising the ovules. These were, however, capable of being fertilised by foreign pollen. In this connection Mendel also mentioned the influence of the environmental conditions on 'sexual weakening or complete sterility'. In his last letter to Nägeli in November 1873 Mendel expressed the belief that

> the naturally occurring hybridisations in *Hieracium* should be ascribed to temporary disturbances, which, if they were repeated often or became permanent, would finally result in the disappearances of the species involved, while one or another of the more happily organised progeny, better adapted to the prevailing telluric and cosmic conditons, might take up the struggle for existence successfully and continue thus for a long period of time, until finally the same fate overtook it.

After 1900 Mendel's friend Niessl, commenting on the experiments with *Hieracium*, which he discussed with Mendel in the experimental garden, recalled Mendel's saying 'my time will come'. To the end of his life Mendel was convinced that his hybridisation research had been correct and that others must reach the same conclusions.

Even when, after the turn of the century, Mendel's research found its way on to the pages of world scientific literature, the only two publications mentioned for a long time were the two concerning peas and hawkweed. It was only much later that a picture emerged of his other research, pieced together from his letters to Nägeli. Scientists were eventually to conclude that, had Mendel published his correspondence, his contemporaries would certainly have taken an interest in his work on plant hybridisation, even though he failed to convince Nägeli himself.

The evolutionary aspect

The question of how Mendel understood evolution, and of his attitude to Darwin's theory, is an interesting one. Answers suggested at one time or another span a whole spectrum of views on the subject, from the assertion that Mendel fully supported the Darwinian concept of evolution to the claim that he totally rejected it. But what any balanced interpretation of Mendel's stance must take into account is the historical development of the natural sciences.

Various theories concerning evolution were published around the middle of the last century, ranging from the speculations of philosophers to those of naturalists. Within the monastery, Mendel knew Bratránek and Klácel, both of whom applied a knowledge of the natural sciences to their philosophical studies. The two monks were interested in extending the ideas of Hegel to the historical sphere. It was Klácel who took the Hegelian concept of a gradual process of development further. He asserted that each phase in the development of each natural phenomenon represented a step in the development of a superior reason. Klácel used examples from the natural sciences to back up his philosophical views; he sought in natural history proof of his philosophy. It was for this reason that he was performing simple experiments in crossing plants at the time when Mendel entered the monastery in 1843, and it may be supposed that through him the younger man became familiar with the notion of dynamism in nature. Klácel saw nature as a process of continuous development, and recommended that the Czech word for it, *příroda*, be replaced by *přeroda*, meaning something like 'nature in flux'.

In his examination essay in geology, written in 1850, Mendel showed he was familiar with Charles Lyell's ideas of evolution in nature. He wrote: 'The Vulcanian and Neptunian formations are not yet completed, for the creative energy of the Earth still remains active. So long as its fires still burn and its atmosphere still moves, the history of creation is not finished.' He referred also to the evolution of living creatures: 'Plant and animal life developed more and more abundantly; the oldest forms disappeared in part, to give way to new, more perfect ones.' Even the idea of the origin of life is contained in the essay: 'As soon as in the course of time the Earth had achieved the necessary capacity for the formation and maintenance of organic life, the first plants and animals of the lowest kinds appeared.' Mendel had most probably read this explanation in Schleiden's book *The Plant and Its Life* (1848), a copy of which is preserved in the monastery library.

While at university Mendel came across the idea of evolution in Unger's lectures. The latter rejected the idea of the constancy of species and advocated research into plant hybridisation, in order to reveal what principles might underlie the variability and development of characters, and even of species. Unger believed that the origin of plant forms must be sought above all in the plants themselves, though he supposed that external influences might bring about modifications. It was just this internal cause of variation which Mendel was seeking. Another aspect of the debate on evolution in the pre-Darwinian era was the unsolved question of the process of procreation, to which Mendel's research was also oriented.

Darwin's name must have come to Mendel's notice, at the latest, in January 1865, in a lecture by Makowsky, though Schwippel, the secretary of the Natural Science Section of the Agricultural Society, had already reported briefly on Darwin's book in 1861. Mendel studied the German translation of *On the Origin of Species*, published in 1863, and acquired the German versions of other books by Darwin. It can be seen from his marginalia how carefully he studied those parts which had a bearing on his research.

Darwin gave natural scientists a far broader picture of the development of nature than any hitherto conceived. He saw nature as a whole, and concentrated on explaining the evolution of living forms from the lowest organisms to the highest, up to man himself. All organisms exhibited variability of characters, and Darwin showed that this organic diversity is a response of the organism to the diversity of the environment. Among the naturally occurring variants, some are better adapted to existing conditions and have more offspring than the less well adapted forms. According to Darwin, evolution operates through the emergence of new forms, differing from the previous ones in minor respects. The force of natural selection favours the better adapted characters and organisms. Darwin was aware that heredity is involved in variability, but had to confess that the laws governing inheritance were completely unknown.

It was this question that Mendel investigated. His field of enquiry was much narrower than Darwin's. He sought to explain the problem of the origin and development of hybrids, and at the same time to contribute to the discussion on the origin of variety and species. His discrete characters were, however, at odds with Darwin's conception of continuous variation, according to which minor changes in characters are constantly occurring, eventually giving rise to new species. Mendel rejected the notion of species stability because, as he put it, it was impossible 'to draw a sharp line between species and varieties' and equally 'between hybrids of species and those of varieties'. He believed that research into plant hybridisation was the key to the problem of the origin of both varieties and species; taking this line, he also refused to accept the influence of the environment on the origin of hybrids. In his *Pisum* paper he mentioned only the names of researchers involved in plant hybridisation. Though he made express reference to the views of noted physiologists, he did not give even Unger's name. One can scarcely wonder, therefore, that he did not mention Darwin. That name does not appear until the *Hieracium* paper of 1870, in connection with Nägeli's views on the transmutation of *Hieracium* species. Three years later, in the letter to Nägeli quoted above (p. 66), Mendel used the Darwinian term 'struggle for existence', accepting this concept as a fact.

Mendel's attitude to Darwin's theory was perhaps best revealed by Niessl, secretary of the Natural Science Society, who later frequently visited Mendel at the monastery. He went on record as saying that Mendel had been 'greatly interested in the idea of evolution, and was far from being an adversary of the Darwinian theory'. Mendel had stated, however, that 'there is still something lacking.' He seems to have meant that Darwin had not explained the essence of that variability on the basis of which natural selection operated. No one, however, knew exactly in what sense Mendel understood all the principles of Darwin's theory.

An innovator in biological research

Mendel embarked upon his experiments in the pre-Darwinian period, when naturalists were chiefly preoccupied with speculation as to whether species were variable or constant, and with the implications of the latest biological research based on the cell theory. Unger was a leading proponent of this research. He himself believed that variations in nature gave rise to new varieties, and possibly also to new species, supposing that some sort of evolution was taking place. When Mendel stepped on to the experimental scene, biological science was teeming with methodological innovations, and new hypotheses, frequently contradictory, were rife. Nägeli had pointed out that new methods bring new discoveries, and these in their turn yet more new methods. The ferment of ideas among naturalists at the time was well characterised by Rudolf Virchow, in 1863:

> In all branches of the organic natural sciences there prevails a state of affairs like that of a country which has undergone deep political upheavals, where all that was previously thought definitive is called into question, where the authorities lose their power, and each is finally left to his own devices.

Such was the situation Mendel found on his return

from Vienna. Convinced, however, that large-scale experiments with plants would provide him with 'much information about their life history', he set about putting his newly acquired learning to work. He must soon have realised that he had hit on something big, that he was giving birth to an entirely new theory, laying the foundation for a completely new line of research. Safe in this assurance, he refused to be discouraged either by the lack of comprehension displayed by his colleagues in Brno or the scepticism of the man he considered the greatest authority on the question, Carl Nägeli. He admitted in his second letter to Nägeli that the cool reception his results had met with came as no surprise to him, and said that he would not have reacted otherwise himself. But he regretted that neither Nägeli nor anyone else had seen fit to repeat the experiments, since he was well aware that his findings were 'not easily compatible with our contemporary scientific knowledge'. Adding what almost amounts to a *cri de cœur*, Mendel commented that performing such experiments in isolation had been 'doubly dangerous: for the experimenter, and for the cause he represented'. Perhaps it is as well that, during his studies and early experiments, Mendel enjoyed both the moral and material support of Abbot Napp, who understood his motivation if anyone did.

Mendel's achievement involved cutting through a mass of irrelevancies in order to combine the most important aspects of recent discoveries about procreation and hybridisation. It was his studies of exact physics which made it possible for him to plan biological research as no one had before. For him the experiments were a means of testing and proving the hypotheses which finally led him to his theory. The experimental inductive work of Mendel the plant breeder interacted with the hypothetico-deductive method of Mendel the physicist, and the result was the fundamental discovery of the physical unit of heredity. His new approach to research consisted chiefly in applying the methods of the physicist, methods ensuring that the same experiment would always produce the same results. He was thus following the recommendation of the Moravian scholar Comenius, who in 1668 exhorted members of the Royal Society of London (whom he addressed as the 'Torch-bearers of this Enlightened Age') to observe the following principles:

> Let your researches into natural objects be so well established, let them bear upon their face so complete an assurance of trustworthiness, that if a man desires not merely to contemplate your work as long as he likes with his unaided eyes, but even to try its accuracy by the most exacting tests of his own device, he shall be certain to find that the facts are precisely what you have shown them to be.

When, after 1900, the *Pisum* experiments were repeated in England and in other countries, it was found that the facts were precisely what Mendel had shown them to be.

5 The abbot and his tragic conflict

In May 1868, Mendel expressed to Nägeli certain misgivings as to the consequences of his election to the abbacy. In the same letter he thanked him for sending further hawkweed seeds, saying that he wanted to obtain hybrids and observe them through several generations—as he had done with peas. As abbot, he was giving up teaching, but he wished to carry on with his scientific work.

A letter to his brother-in-law in his native village suggests that Mendel did want to be elected abbot, since the appointment carried with it, in addition to ecclesiastical and social status, a considerable income. The latter enabled him to provide for his sister Theresia's three sons to go to university—a fitting way of repaying her generosity in financing his own studies during the difficult days at Olomouc.

Mendel was taking up the post which Napp had occupied for the last forty-three years—a period, except for 1848, of relative political stability. Napp had held, simultaneously, positions of eminence in public institutions such as the provincial assembly, in learned societies and in organisations of a cultural and social character. He was recognised for the breadth of his education and exceptional organising ability. Mendel was expected to be heir to his secular domain as well as to his ecclesiastical duties.

Voting in the abbatial elections ran into three rounds. The only other candidate was Thomas Bratránek, but he was already a professor at the University of Cracow, and was loath to renounce the post. At this time there were roughly equal numbers of Czechs and Germans in the monastery. Mendel's greatest asset as a candidate was his placid disposition and modest manner. Owing much of his support to his considerable standing as a Gymnasium teacher and a member of learned societies, he seemed to have the makings of a second Napp. However, those very attributes of personality which made Mendel popular among naturalists were to prove more of a disadvantage than an asset in his new role, and this was to have an impact not only on the internal calm of the community, but also on the monastery's economic affairs.

Politics and public life

Mendel took over the abbacy at a time of major political change. In the previous year, 1867, the Habsburg Monarchy had been transformed from a autocratic state into the Austro-Hungarian constitutional monarchy. Equal rights were granted to the German and Hungarian ruling classes, but the situation of the underprivileged ethnic minorities, especially the Czechs, remained unresolved. The moving force behind the provisions of the new constitution was the liberal party, which operated from a platform of Germano-Hungarian hegemony. The opposition conservative party mainly comprised the big landowners and the members of the ecclesiastical hierarchy, and it was with them that the political leaders of the oppressed national groups threw in their lot. The new government introduced a number of reforms. Legal questions relating to family matters passed from the jurisdiction of the Church to that of the State, and the State also took over responsibility for schools. These measures stirred up opposition in Church circles.

As abbot of a monastery with a large estate, Mendel was a delegate to the Provincial Assembly. To the great surprise of all concerned, in the 1870 and 1871 elections to the assembly he came out in support of the constitutional party, which the Czech majority in Moravia regarded as the embodiment of German nationalism. The other representatives of ecclesiastical institutions supported the conservatives, as had Abbot Napp. In September 1871, a protest was read in the assembly on behalf of the delegates of the constitutional party, against the illegal procedure adopted during the election of one of the members of the conservative party; Mendel was among the signatories. This increased still further animosity towards him, which was already rife among the members of the conservative party, and particularly at the Bishop's Office in Brno.

The Czechs in the Augustinian community came to regard the abbot as their political adversary. Mendel's political gesture had consequences more far-reaching than he seemed to realise. He may have been motivated by his class origins and his critical attitude to the vestiges of that feudalism which he personally had been forced to overcome in his struggle to gain an education. A further factor must have been the liberal atmosphere of the Realschule where he had taught for fourteen years. Mendel's former superior at the school, Auspitz, was by now a prominent political figure, and played a major role in constitutional party politics from 1870. It was on his proposal that the provincial governor nominated Mendel in the spring of 1872 for the Order of Franz Josef, a high State honour. The nomination was rapidly confirmed, and the published citation for the award referred to Mendel's political service, and his previous successful career as a teacher at the Realschule.

Following his election to the abbacy, Mendel was also elected, at the end of 1868, to the post of vice-president of the Natural Science Society. Then the focus of his activities shifted to his new position as a committee member in the Agricultural Society. From 1872 he was entrusted with the vice-presidency, as Napp had been before him. Whereas Napp's role in the society had been largely that of organiser, Mendel's was more that of an expert natural scientist.

His duties—sitting on various boards of experts—were an obstacle to his continuing research, and he began to attend Natural Science Society meetings less often. He devoted a considerable amount of time to the distribution of government subsidies to agriculture. Having taken on the task of organising the statistical processing of reports on agricultural production, he stated the case for increasing subsidies for collecting information, in order to ensure the reliability of statistical estimates. His interest in professional publications led him to publish brief reviews of the latest books published on relevant subjects. He also took a hand in the editorial work of the society journal, and gave his opinion on prize essays.

The surviving records of the deliberations of the Agricultural Society committee show the breadth of the activities in which Mendel made use of his expert knowledge. It was this professional competence which ensured his repeated re-election to the committee, even though a growing dispute with the State authorities regarding taxation of the monastery meant that there were those who began to cast their votes against him. Still, he always got the necessary majority. When, in 1882, he was offered the presidency of the society, he declined on the grounds of increasing ill-health.

Eminent horticulturist

Mendel showed an increasing interest in the cultivation of plant varieties. In 1859 he had exhibited newly obtained varieties of pumpkin; no details of the manner in which they were obtained have, however, been preserved. He joined the Horticultural Section the following year. He was already co-operating with one of its leading members, Tvrdý, and visited him frequently to discuss problems in the garden and greenhouse. During the 1860s, Brno horticulturists devoted considerable effort to the selection of flowers. Tvrdý was widely known as a producer of many flower varieties which found their way into the major cities of Europe. He made a name for himself in particular as a breeder of fuchsias, which he liked to name after leading political figures and natural scientists, such as Galileo and Alexander Humboldt. Interestingly, one fuchsia was given the name 'Evolution'. He also called one variety 'Prelate Mendel', in acknowledgement of his co-operation with a scientist for whose expertise he had the highest regard.

Mendel too took great pleasure in selecting flowers, and had marked a passage in Gärtner's monograph on plant breeding describing the possibility of obtaining varieties with new colours by means of artificial crossing. He was also interested in the selective breeding of vines, as was Napp before him. Even his experiments with peas produced practical results: one of the types he obtained was outstanding from the culinary point of view, and was sown in the monastery vegetable garden.

Most of his horticultural efforts, however, were absorbed in the cultivation of fruit trees. For his new varieties of apple and pear trees he was awarded the Medal of the Hietzing Horticultural Society in Vienna. In 1882 the first prize awarded for a new variety of pear tree at the Brno show was not collected by the anonymous exhibitor, who seems to have been Mendel. The monastery gardener later claimed that during Mendel's abbacy between five and six hundred pear, apple and apricot seedlings were grown in the Augustinians' garden.

We have in Brno notes written by Mendel in pomological publications, some of them outlining the crossing of various varieties of apple and pear trees. According to these, Mendel considered crossing twelve maternal and seventeen pollen varieties in thirty combinations. His main aim was to combine flavour characteristics with resistance to adverse climatic and soil conditions. The apple of best flavour was only obtainable under warm conditions and in a rich soil. In less favourable conditions the taste was inferior. The pollen variety produced apples with a mediocre flavour, but it blossomed later and was less sensitive to cooler weather and poorer soil. In other combinations Mendel intended to put together the flavour characteristics of the original varieties. Other outstanding pomologists in Europe were making similar efforts, and Mendel followed their results eagerly in specialised publications.

The last information we have on Mendel's plant crossing experiments relates to the selection of apple and pear trees. A year before his death he wrote to his brother-in-law in his native village, asking him to send grafts of fruit-tree varieties from his late father's garden—presumably those which Anton Mendel had obtained from the parish priest, Fr. Schreiber. 'What a gardener our prelate was!' recalled the monastery gardener, Mareš, who took his instructions from the abbot himself. 'There is not a single gardener who could not have learned from him!' Long after Mendel's death there were still trees in the monastery garden bearing metal tags put there during his abbacy.

Research in apiculture

Abbot Napp had been anxious to promote beekeeping throughout the province, and had managed to organise an Apicultural Society which, at the time Mendel was made abbot, was the biggest in central Europe. In 1868 there were 1,200 members in the society and its activities were directed by a retired doctor, František Živanský (1817–73). Mendel joined in 1870, and soon acquired a reputation in apicultural research. He had an experimental apiary constructed at the monastery, from which the first institute of apicultural research in the province was to develop. In Moravia at the time the keeping of foreign breeds was recommended, on the grounds that they were more productive. Mendel, however, kept various breeds, even those from which he could expect no practical benefit. His interest in them stemmed from his research, and he carried out a critical assessment of the advantages and disadvantages of individual races. He made detailed records of, for example, swarming, energy in flight and nuptial flights, and the external morphological characters of the bees. He used the same approach as with the characters of plants during his crossing experiments. The journal of the Apicultural Society noted in 1876 that 'The Most Reverend Herr Prelate intends to breed a new, synthetic race by means of artificial crossing.' But he had a number of complex problems to overcome. First he tried the controlled mating of queens with selected drones. In front of the experimental hive he had a cage constructed according to his own design (4 × 4 × 33 mm), covered with gauze. The queen was able to fly in, but the workers could not.

He soon found, however, that it was not possible to achieve fertilisation by this method, since the drones fertilise the queen in flight, at a considerable height, at least ten metres.

Mendel kept races which differed in appearance, in order to keep a check on the results of crossing bees with different characters. He reported that his bees flew quite far, up to several kilometres: he could show that, for example, a Cyprian drone from Brno had fertilised a queen from Liskovec, about five kilometres away. In 1876 he also noted increased resilience and fertility in hybrids (a Cyprian queen and a domestic drone) from two families. This, he asserted, 'could not be the product of chance'.

Later in his research on bees Mendel concentrated on studying the conditions under which they wintered, the optimum pasture for them, and the health of the swarm. In 1879 a swarm of South American bees was fortuitously brought to Brno, and Mendel attempted to breed them. It was a stingless race, which Mendel identified as *Trigona lineata*. French beekeepers had already tried to breed this species, but the bees soon died, being sensitive to European climatic conditions. Mendel had a warm-water heating system made for them, and in this way he managed to keep the bees from July 1879 to February of the following year. He made meticulous observations of their attributes, and handed the results over to his friend Anton Tomaschek, who published them in 1879 and 1880 in two extensive contributions to the journal *Zoologischer Anzeiger* in Leipzig. A third, shorter report Tomaschek sent to Moscow, where zoologists were interested in problems of the acclimatisation of animals and in apiculture. It was not published until 1885, after Mendel's death. The article stresses

that Abbot Mendel was a leading researcher in the field
of apiculture.

Mendel may have met leading European beekeepers as
far back as 1865. In that year a congress of German
apiculturists was held in Brno, with about 300 participants from all over central Europe. Among them were a
Silesian beekeeper who was at the time famous, Jan
Dzierzon, and Gustav Dathe. Both were Abbot Napp's
guests at the monastery. When the 1871 congress of
apiculturists was held in Kiel, Živanský attended as
president of the society and Mendel as vice-president,
visiting Dathe at Eystrup on the way. At Kiel, Živanský
was asked to prepare the constitution of an international
apicultural organisation; unfortunately, he soon fell seriously ill, and in 1873 he died. The officials of the Apicultural Society offered the presidency to Mendel, but he
declined. Apparently he did not consider himself an
organiser of Živanský's calibre, and preferred to occupy
himself with natural science and with research.

The meteorologist

In the years between 1854 and 1873 Mendel had carried
out intensive research into plant hybridisation. He
began his apicultural research in 1871, and devoted his
efforts to it, when his health permitted, to the end of his
life. But it was to meteorology that he consecrated his
attention over the longest period of all. From 1856 he
processed the results of meteorological observations.
This led him to make his own observations, and he
continued to do so till the last days of his life.

Pioneer work on meteorology had been done in Bohemia by Johannes Kepler, who spent the years between
1600 and 1612 in Prague. At the end of the eighteenth
century interest in the subject spread throughout Bohe-

mia and into neighbouring Moravia. In his programme of scientific progress in 1806, André had emphasised the importance of regular observations, and in 1816 he drew up the constitution of a meteorological society, based in Brno. From then on its members made observations in several towns and published the results. In 1849 the activities of this society were transferred to the Natural Science Section of the Agricultural Society, and from 1862 to the newly formed independent Natural Science Society. From 1846 the observations in Brno were made by Olexík, on whose suggestion Mendel began in 1856 to process the results.

While Mendel was studying at the Gymnasium in Opava, one of the teachers there, Faustin Ens, carried out meteorological observations, and published the results in appropriate form. The physics professor at Olomouc, Franz, who proposed Mendel's admission to the Brno monastery, also dabbled in meteorology. At the monastery the young Mendel met Fr. Gabriel, teacher of mathematics at the Těsín grammar school, who also made observations. Another amateur meteorologist was Zawadski, whom Mendel met at the Realschule in 1854. There can be no doubt that acquaintance with these people nurtured Mendel's interest in the subject. Later, in 1857, Mendel's name was mentioned in connection with meteorology in a list of seventeen specialists in various branches of natural science, who were to deal in Brno with questions from the public.

In the field of meteorology Mendel also co-operated with Carl Fritsch, at whose instigation the Austrian Meteorological Society was set up in 1865. After his election as abbot, Mendel became a founder-member. Previously, in 1861 and 1862, he had carried out phenological observations in Brno, which Fritsch had published. Mendel's co-operation with Olexík gradually developed into independent meteorological observations which he undertook at the monastery. In Olexík's absence Mendel made his observations for him, and at a meeting in 1862 he lectured to the Natural Science Society on meteorological observations made in Brno between 1848 and 1862. In the following year the lecture was published in the society's proceedings, together with graphs of temperature, humidity, air pressure, wind direction and strength, precipitation and ozone level. Fluctuations were expressed on the basis of a five-day mean. Mendel made a comparison between the data for individual years and the means for the previous fifteen years, thus underlining the importance of statistical evaluation in meteorology. Later he regularly published the results of meteorological observations from all Moravian stations. The last time he did so was in 1869. The published data were accompanied by an astute commentary. He noted, for example, the effect of urban exhalations on the ozone level and on temperatures. In 1864 he mentioned observations of the height of the water table, and later he also made a systematic record of the level of the water in the monastery well.

Mendel's most remarkable meteorological material was that presented at a lecture to the Natural Science Society in 1870. He was fascinated by a freak whirlwind which hit Brno on 13 October of that year, and whose passage he observed from an open window. Following a noisy blast of wind, accompanied by a rattling of windows and loosening of slates, a black pillar in the shape of a double cone appeared, reminding Mendel of an hourglass. He estimated the height of the upper cone at about 300 metres, that of the lower at 230 metres. The column spun in a clockwise direction, which Mendel considered an exception to the general rule applicable to such phenomena in the northern hemisphere. He put the width of the whirlwind's base at between one and two hundred metres, and, making a comparison with an express train, estimated its forward speed at 135–170 km/h. The whirlwind caused great damage to roofs and chimneys in the town. In the second part of his study, Mendel accurately described the manner in which such atmospheric disturbances arise from a meeting of two airstreams travelling in different directions and having different characteristics. His description of the whirlwind demonstrates Mendel's scientific enthusiasm for special natural phenomena and his exceptional observational talent. What he himself had seen, supplemented by the evidence of other eyewitnesses, led him to attempt to create a theory on the origin and course of the whirlwind. After twenty-six days Mendel was ready to report on this topic and had also prepared an extensive seventeen-page paper, which was published later.

Mendel also tried to put the results of meteorological observations to practical use. Back in 1850, in the written part of the teachers' examination, he had, in describing the mechanical and chemical properties of the atmosphere, pointed out the importance of taking meteorological observations in several places at once, and suggested that telegraphy might be exploited in the rapid distribution of weather data. This in fact was done at the end of the 1870s, and there was then a suggestion that weather forecasts be issued during the harvest. Mendel gave his expert opinion on the proposal, and it also was published. He stressed that there was a real possibility of making use of scientific knowledge in order to predict the weather.

In the early 1870s meteorologists in Kodani began to

issue summaries of meteorological observations from various stations in Europe. Mendel obtained these, and on the basis of his assessment of them he published in Brno in 1879, under the initial 'M', a discussion of the possibility of issuing weather forecasts. He approved attempts to publish such forecasts based on the analysis of observations from several different places, and denounced the still-current practice of predicting the weather according to a hundred-year calendar. He drew attention to the fact that the meteorological situation in central Europe was an extremely complex one, making forecasting there particularly difficult. There were, he pointed out, over a hundred weather stations in the United States, while in Europe meteorologists had only the data of some twenty or thirty stations available to them. Echoing his remarks on the hybridisation of plants, he emphasised the importance of making as large a number of observations as was practically possible: these would form the basis of an analysis from which a forecast could then be made.

Towards the end of his life, Abbot Mendel devoted his attention more and more to meteorology. Surviving records of his observations, which are accompanied by extensive comments, show how thoroughly he kept them, almost to his dying day. In his final years he procured an astronomical telescope and studied the occurrence of sunspots, with a view to improving weather forecasting; here, however, he was unsuccessful. Records of his own observations are the only surviving evidence of his research efforts in this sphere.

Mendel became an acknowledged authority on meteorology, not only in Brno, but as a member of the Vienna Meteorological Society. He had many friends among experts on the subject. One of these was the

Professor of Meteorology at Vienna, Josef Líznar, an ex-pupil of the Brno Realschule. Only a few days before his death Mendel sent Líznar a letter in which he complained of heart trouble, which, he said, made it impossible for him to read his meteorological instruments without assistance. 'Since we are unlikely to meet again in this world,' Mendel wrote, 'let me take this opportunity of wishing you farewell, and of invoking upon your head all the blessings of the meteorological deities.'

Conflict

While striving to fulfil his duties as abbot as best he could, Mendel took every opportunity to study the literature of natural science, purchasing a large number of books and, towards the end of his life, becoming more and more absorbed in astronomy and meteorology. Before he had held office very long, however, the new abbot came to realise that his hopes of having more free time for research were ill-founded. His disappointment is expressed in his letters to Nägeli. In the last, dated 18 November 1873, he bemoaned the fact that the hawk-weed had 'withered again without my having been able to pay them more than a few hurried visits'. He sent Nägeli details of his experiments with these plants in 1870–1, admitting that he was unsure whether he would be able to continue with them the following year. Nägeli was impressed with the results, and replied in a letter dated 23 June 1874. When he received no response, he sent another letter the following year, but Mendel never answered it. Questions of the management of the monastery and its estates were by now taking up more and more of his time, and he was probably preoccupied with problems arising from his political stand in 1871, the consequences of which were coming to a head in 1874.

In that year the Habsburg government, formed by the ruling constitutional party, published draft legislation increasing the tax levied on monastic property to offset government expenditure on ecclesiastical institutions. The law was to take effect from the start of the following year. The Brno monastery was assessed at 7,330 guilders per annum. When the bill was debated, the representatives of the Church and the conservative party delegates expressed their opposition to the new provisions, but eventually agreed to abide by them. The only abbot in the whole of the Monarchy who flatly refused to accept them was Gregor Mendel. He started to study legal sources, and set out to find some way of justifying his rejection of the law. The Czech members of his community were not slow to remind him that the law was the work of the constitutional party, to whom the abbot had lent his support.

In this politically and legally complex situation, Mendel steadfastly refused to take the advice of lawyers, and tried stubbornly to find some alternative interpretation of the law. When the tax fell due, he offered 'as a gesture of good will' to pay a mere 2,000 guilders. Local officials forwarded his protest to the central authorities in Vienna for attention. They received an uncompromising reply, requiring them to discharge their duty of collecting in full. In 1876 the State authorities seized part of the monastery properties and enforced payment of the tax.

Mendel felt humiliated by this latest move, and responded by stepping up his opposition to the law. His obstinate attitude became an embarrassment to the constitutional party in Brno. At this stage Dr Auspitz tried to take a hand. As editor of the influential party daily newspaper, he was in touch with leading party officials. A new mortgage bank was being set up in Brno at the time, and Mendel had been offered the post of assistant director. When, in 1881, the director, Dr Ott, died, he took over the senior post. He used the income from the appointment to finance his nephews' studies, to pay scientific subscriptions, and for the relief of poverty. He did not, however, make any concessions in his stance towards the ecclesiastical taxation law.

In his unrelenting defiance of the authorities, Mendel refused to pay any heed even to the views of the monastery's lawyer. As late as 1882 he sought the opinion of an expert on constitutional law from Prague, who explained to him at some length that he had no choice but to respect the provisions of the law. Even this failed to make any impression on the abbot, who remained unwilling to pay the tax to the end of his life. Certain that he was right, and determined to persevere (just as in the pea experiments), Mendel spent nine years studying the legal situation and writing one letter of protest after another, all of which met with a blank wall of indifference. His health began to decline, and he grew more and more mistrustful even of those nearest to him.

Last days

Since his election to the abbacy, Mendel had been host to many visitors at the monastery. Among them were representatives of ecclesiastical and State institutions, his former colleagues from the schools he had taught in, and his friends from the Natural Science Society and the other scientific bodies to which he belonged. In summer he would receive them in the monastery gardens, where the orangery, adapted as a horticultural laboratory, served as a summerhouse. There was a bowling-alley nearby. Mendel like to play chess, and would think up new problems to set his nephews, who were his most frequent visitors. As abbot he supported cultural institutions, but did not himself participate in the cultural life of the town.

When he voted for the liberal party in 1870 and 1871, Mendel won friends and supporters in public life, though his courageous political stand cost him the favour of some of his ecclesiastical associates. His subsequent dispute with the authorities, however, led to his virtual isolation, and he sought refuge mainly in the study of scientific works. He was no longer able to undertake exacting experiments in plant crossing, but he cultivated some varieties for his own pleasure. In 1878 he was visited by C. W. Eichling, the representative of a French seed producer, who wished to discover the extent to which Mendel's experiments had found a practical application. Mendel is said to have shown him his beds of peas, which he had 'reshaped in height as well as in the type of fruit'. When asked how he had achieved this, he replied: 'It is just a little trick, but there is a long story connected with it, which would take too long to tell.' He avoided further talk about the *Pisum* experiments and changed the subject, inviting Eichling to see beds of well-grown vegetables and trees loaded with fruit.

Eichling published his reminiscences of his visit to Abbot Mendel only after many years had elapsed—in 1942. His customer in Brno in 1878 had apparently been of the opinion that Mendel's experiments with *Pisum* were no more than a pastime. Eichling's comments show that the great man was at least known for his research work, which was recognised as being very demanding; no one, however, grasped the far-reaching significance of what he was doing.

At the time of Eichling's visit to the monastery, Mendel must have been affected by the gathering storm-clouds of conflict with the State authorities. His friend Olexík was ill, and the abbot had taken over responsibility for the Brno weather station. His interest was shifting towards meteorology. Fragments of the abbot's records of the occurrence of sunspots show that he spent hours sitting at his telescope, and made a painstaking graph of his observations. He began to feel more and more lonely, and his state of health steadily deteriorated.

The dispute over the ecclesiastical tax placed the obstinate abbot in ever-increasing isolation, not only from public life, but even within the monastery itself. Around this time Mendel had the ceiling of the reception room in his quarters painted with scenes chosen by himself. In the centre was a portrait of St Augustine with his mother St Monica, symbolising Mendel's faith and the Augustinian order. The motifs at the four corners reflected his scientific interests. One shows two men grafting fruit trees. In the background is a hamlet at the foot of a hill, easily identifiable as Vražné, near Mendel's birthplace. The orchard in the painting is located at the spot where Schreiber, the parish priest, had his fruit-tree nursery. A second painting depicts a beehive known as Dzierzon's double hive, together with an old straw beehive. This motif represents the modernisation of bee-keeping, to which Mendel's research had contributed. In the third corner are a telescope, globe, compass and thermometer, symbolising the abbot's involvement in meteorology. The final painting is of the kneeling figure of St Isidor, patron saint of agriculture—possibly an echo of Mendel's peasant origins. These themes represent the most significant spheres of Mendel's activity, the things he considered part of his mission in life. Here in his quarters he found privacy; he built a world within a world, a refuge in his troubled years.

A surviving letter to his relatives in his native village shows Mendel's warm feelings towards his home, to which his thoughts would often return. In his capacity as abbot he donated 3,000 guilders to equip the village fire station. The building stands to this day, and bears a memorial plaque unveiled in 1902, two years after the 'rediscovery' of Mendel's classic paper.

A source of great pleasure to Mendel was his regular contact with his nephews, Ferdinand and Alois Schindler, who attended the Gymnasium in Brno and later went on to study medicine in Vienna. He was able to discuss his failing health with these young medical students, who, he felt, were the only friends who had not deserted him. He tried to overcome his inner tensions by smoking large numbers of cigars, though his doctors had warned him against it. Finally, with stoic resignation, he awaited the end. As the shadow of approaching death lay heavy on him, he asked that a post-mortem be carried out on his body. Exhausted, he died in his sleep on the night of the Epiphany, 6 January 1884, at the age of sixty-one. The doctor recorded the cause of death as inflammation of the kidneys, accompanied by cardiac hypertrophy.

The funeral was attended by representatives of Church and State, and both Mendel's work and his personality were praised. The newspaper of the constitutional party declared that in the deceased the poor had lost a benefactor and mankind a most noble character, a cordial friend of the natural sciences, and an exemplary priest. But perhaps the most fitting tribute was that paid by the secretary of the Natural Science Society, Niessl.

Describing Mendel's passing as an irreplaceable loss, he recalled that the abbot had spent every spare moment his fortunate position afforded 'almost exclusively on detailed natural scientific studies, in which he displayed a totally independent, unique way of thinking'. Niessl, who was himself incapable of understanding Mendel's work, none the less recognised the originality of his approach.

In another newspaper, an anonymous obituary pointed out how much research Mendel had published, especially in meteorology, under the auspices of the Natural Science Society. The obituary ends by noting his 'research with plant hybrids'. Horticulturists, however, in an obituary appreciating Mendel's breeding of new varieties of fruit-trees and flowers went so far as to write that 'his experiments in plant hybridisation were epoch-making', and would never be forgotten.

Exploiting fully the opportunities offered by the monastic life, the late abbot had devoted himself to the study of natural science and the pursuit of truth. Mendel's path was not a straightforward one; yet shortly before his death a future abbot of the monastery, Fr. F. Bařina, heard him recall:

> Though I have suffered some bitter moments in my life, I must thankfully admit that most of it has been pleasant and good. My scientific work has brought me a great deal of satisfaction, and I am convinced that it will not be long before the whole world acknowledges it.

6 Belated recognition

Up to the centenary of the *Pisum* paper's publication in 1965, it was usually said to have remained in almost total obscurity until the end of the nineteenth century, only referred to by two or three authors. But it is now known that Mendel's work was quoted relatively frequently by botanists from 1867 onwards. As early as 1869, the German botanist H. Hoffmann paid considerable attention to it in a monograph where he stated that Mendel had obtained hybrids from constant forms and that they 'had a tendency to revert in subsequent generations to the parental forms'. Hoffmann's study brought Mendel's research to the attention of the German botanist W. O. Focke, who referred to it in a monograph of his own in 1881, in connection with *Pisum*, *Phaseolus* and *Hieracium* hybrids. Focke claimed that the *Pisum* experiments had produced results entirely similar to those published by T. A. Knight. He went on to say how Mendel believed he had discovered 'constant ratios between various types of hybrid'. Charles Darwin lent a copy of Focke's book to G. J. Romanes, who as a result cited Mendel's work in the *Encyclopaedia Britannica*; Darwin himself, however, took no notice of the mention of Mendel's work in the book.

In 1872 A. Blomberg was also to refer to the *Pisum* paper, in a dissertation on plant hybrids published in Swedish. He mentioned Mendel's exposition of the segregation of characters in the hybrid progeny and his rejection of the idea that hybrids were sometimes constant. Two years later I. F. Shmalgausen in St Petersburg, in a dissertation on plant hybrids, noted Mendel's mathematical evaluation of the occurrence of various characters in the hybrid progeny. In fact both Mendel's papers were already referred to quite frequently in botanical literature. They were included in a catalogue of scientific literature published in 1879 in England. In 1890 L. H. Bailey in the United States referred to them in connection with the crossing and selection of plants. This line of research led a number of workers, towards the turn of the century, to concentrate their attention on plant hybridisation and to quote Mendel's publications.

Mendel's work was thus not completely neglected before 1900. Some botanists investigating hybrid plants from the standpoint of taxonomy or evolution did refer to it. They quoted Mendel's hybridising paper, but we do not know whether they read it. Nägeli was the one best placed to make an in-depth appraisal of what Mendel had achieved, because, in addition to the reprints, Mendel sent him ten letters containing information about his experiments with other plant species. The quotation of Mendel's papers by Hoffman and Focke led Blomberg and Shmalgausen to study the *Pisum* paper, and they underlined some aspects of Mendel's methodological innovation. Their remarks, however, passed unnoticed.

So it was that the significance of Mendel's research remained unappreciated till 1900. One reason why little attention was paid to his publications might have been that in the world of scientific literature his name was unknown. Another contributory cause of his being overlooked may have been the fact that in the second of his major publications, the *Hieracium* paper of 1871, he did not confirm the theory elaborated for *Pisum*.

After becoming abbot, Mendel lacked the time and energy to continue his research. He was soon only too well aware of this, which is why he somewhat prematurely published the initial results of his further research, devoted mainly to the most complex problems of heredity, with the genus *Hieracium*. He sent the details to Nägeli and was to find that this eminent botanist, though interested in the research, was incapable of appreciating its true significance. Mendel found himself out on a limb. While he had been teaching physics and natural history he had at least been able to discuss the question with his colleagues, but as abbot he had lost regular contact with natural scientists. None the less, in 1870 he was continuing his research to a limited extent, and in 1873 wrote to Nägeli of new results, which, had he published them, might have attracted more notice among the readers of scientific journals than the *Hieracium* paper did. He never replied to the last letters Nägeli sent him, in 1873 and 1875, though the latter's keen interest in his work might have been seen as a compliment. It was a time of great upheaval in Mendel's life.

It must be borne in mind that Mendel carried out his research in his spare time, inspired only by a personal devotion to science. He had no scientific collaborators in his research and, as a private scholar, no pupils to carry on where he left off. Though he had friends in Brno who were natural scientists and who were also interested in the hybridisation of plants, not one among them possessed facilities like an experimental garden or experimental glass-house that were necessary for such exacting research. Nor did they have the time, or, most important of all, the extraordinary motivation which Mendel had. None of those who studied his work at the end of the last century, taking an interest in hybridisation from the taxonomical or evolutionary angle, had Mendel's broad knowledge of natural science. Thus they all failed to see the originality of method and results in his *Pisum* work, and understood his research only to a limited extent.

During the second half of the nineteenth century, the study of heredity became the object of renewed interest on account of Darwin's theory and, later, of advances in cytology (the branch of biology dealing with the cell). Darwin had discussed the transfer of characters in an extensive 1868 monograph entitled *The Variation of Animals and Plants under Domestication*. He put forward the provisional hypothesis of 'pangenesis', whereby heredity involved the transfer of special units called 'gemmules', which assembled in the reproductive cells from all parts of the body. This was a spur to naturalists to investigate the determinants of heredity. Nägeli, following this line of research, published in 1884 a monograph on the mechanical and physiological theory of development, putting forward his own notion of 'idioplasm', what he supposed to be the generative portion of a cell as distinct from the vegetative portion. He stated that plant characters were determined in the cell by special molecular units which, like Mendel, he called in German *Anlage*. Nägeli even described dominant and latent characters, though never mentioning Mendel's name in this connection. With his belief in a distinct 'idioplasm' as the hereditary substance, Nägeli significantly influenced the thinking of his contemporaries.

Further progress was made by the German zoologist August Weismann, who adopted the idea of 'idioplasm' in his speculative theory of the constancy of germ plasm. According to him this plasm could be the bearer of heredity. Hugo de Vries was soon to expand the pangenesis theory, asserting that characters were inherited through units called 'pangenes' in the nucleus of the cell. He crossed plants differing in various pairs of characters, seeking proof of this theory. In the years 1892–6 de Vries observed segregation of characters in the ratio 3:1. He published some of his results in 1899, but his main work on the subject was published in 1900; there he expressed his conclusions in the form of a generally applicable Law of Segregation, which he attributed to Mendel.

De Vries's paper prompted Carl Correns (1864–1935) to bring forward publication of the results of his own experiments with plant hybridisation. He had been investigating the visible effect of certain kinds of pollen on the colour characteristics of the seed. Mendel's principle was mentioned in the title of his paper, and at the end of it Correns formulated principles of dominance and segregation. In the same journal where de Vries and Correns published their work, a third paper on the artificial crossing of peas appeared in 1900. The author was Erich von Tschermak (1871–1962), who was studying the hybrid effect in plant crosses. He had been spurred on to early publication by the appearance of the papers by de Vries and Correns. Describing the progeny of hybrids, Tschermak referred to a segregation ratio of 'about three to one', and noted at the end of his work that he was able to confirm what Mendel propounded.

Then attention was drawn to Mendel's paper by the English biologist William Bateson (1861–1926). Influenced by Darwin's interpretation of the continuous variation of characters in plants and animals, he studied plant hybridisation in conjunction with the phenomena of variation, heredity and evolution. In 1899, in a published lecture on plant hybridisation as a method of research, Bateson recommended using statistical methods to investigate the characters of parents, hybrids and subsequent progeny. In 1900 his attention was drawn to Mendel's work by de Vries's paper. He immediately returned to the results he had obtained for poultry hybrids and examined them anew in the light of Mendel's methods. Soon he was to become one of the most prominent pioneers of the new science of heredity.

The year 1900 thus came to be known as the date of the 'rediscovery' of Mendel's work by de Vries, Correns and Tschermak. We can now assume that de Vries and Correns were aware of Mendel's *Pisum* paper before they completed their own experiments. They arranged their research accordingly and offered explanations of the results which tied in with Mendel's conclusions. Of the three, Tschermak had the most tenuous grasp of the essence of Mendel's theory, but he was eventually to make his mark in connection with its practical application in plant breeding.

When, in the last decades of the nineteenth century, the full impact of Darwin's theory of evolution came to be felt, and cytology revealed the mechanism of cell division and the fertilisation process in the behaviour of the morphological structures of the nucleus, called *chromosomes*, T. Boveri was led to speculate on the connection between chromosomes and heredity. This connection was even more strongly stated by E. B. Wilson in 1896. At that time, however, such ideas were far from meeting with universal approval. It was only the study of Mendel's theory which, in 1903, convincingly linked chromosomes with heredity.

When attention was focused on Mendel's publications, a growing number of biologists began to examine the question of heredity. They used the crossing methods, symbols and statistical evaluation introduced by Mendel. The publication of his work in foreign languages gave further impetus to the search. Scientific progress made the task of the biologists easier, and soon the trail led not only through the realm of plants and animals, but to man himself, and on into the strange world of the micro-organism.

As frequently happens in the march of science, however, the general acceptance of Mendel's theory threw up new obstacles, arising from an incomplete understanding of what actual progress had been made, and particularly from the difficulties encountered in harmonising the new science of genetics with existing knowledge of evolution, and of biology in general. Bateson campaigned for the establishment of Mendelism, opposing Darwin's concept of continuous variation. This sparked off a major dispute, first in England, and later in other countries. Proponents of continuous variation and its significance in the evolutionary process rejected the general validity of Mendel's theory. They based their standpoint on biometrical studies of character variation, particularly of characters with a quantitative character, whose heredity the Mendelians were unable to explain.

Shortly after the 'rediscovery', Hugo de Vries published a theory of *mutation*, by means of which he explained the sudden appearance of new characters. De Vries supposed that mutation and character combination might actually give rise to new species. This provoked a new debate. It was soon shown that, contrary to what Mendel supposed in 1865, not all characters are governed by a single hereditary unit (or, after 1909, gene), but that some characters are determined by several. Then the difficulties between Darwinists and Mendelians began to be elucidated in terms of the frequency of genes and gene combinations, exploiting the theory of mutation. This led eventually, in the 1920s, to the harmonising of genetics with the theory of evolution, and an end to the arguments as to whether Darwin or Mendel had been right. This step, known as the synthesis of the two theories, opened the way to the investigation of further problems of heredity that concerned the very essence, origin and development of living systems.

A major contribution to the synthesis of heredity and evolution was made by the Cambridge statistician R. A. Fisher, who in 1936 made an analysis of Mendel's *Pisum* work. He first had to reconstruct the individual experiments, and he came to the conclusion that the numerical data relating to the plants and seeds were 'too good to be true', from the point of view of statistical significance. Fisher explained this by suggesting that Mendel knew the theoretical ratios of character segregation before he began his experiments, and that consequently some assistant might have cooked the numerical data to fit the expected ratios. Other voices were raised which suggested that Mendel himself might have 'adjusted' the data to fit the theory. But in 1966 the biometrician Franz Weiling pointed out the fallacy of Fisher's assumption that, out of ten seeds from plants tested for constancy, Mendel obtained ten plants. In fact the germination rate of the seeds had to be taken into account. Assuming, as experience would indicate, a germination rate of some 90 per cent, Weiling recalculated the probability of Mendel's result, and matched the data from repeats of the experiments described by various researchers since 1900. This would seem to have removed the last shadow of doubt as to the credibility of Mendel's experiments and his published results.

A great impact was made on the twentieth-century development of genetics by the rise of cytology. In 1903 W. S. Sutton recommended that heredity be studied in connection with chromosomes. This led T. H. Morgan (1877–1945) and his colleagues to produce the chromosome theory of heredity, introducing the new experimental model *Drosophila melanogaster* (the fruit fly). Genes were 'mapped', i.e. their location on the chromosome was determined. One of the members of Morgan's school was J. M. Müller (1890–1967), who discovered in 1927 the possibility of inducing mutations by means of X-rays, thus lending a new impetus to genetic research.

After the Second World War, the exploration of genetics took off, involving both biochemists and biophysicists. Mendel had merely proved the existence of units of heredity. After 1910 the idea was put forward that the gene might consist specifically of an enzyme, or a substance which produced enzymes, but it was many years before geneticists were in a position to investigate its chemical nature. In 1944 the physicist Erwin Schrödinger expressed the conviction that the hereditary units would be identified through physics, on the basis of new developments in biochemistry, 'under the guidance of physiology and genetics'. Soon afterwards, the carriers of heredity were shown to be the nucleic acids, which had been discovered by J. F. Miescher (1844–95) in the last century. In 1895, the rector of Prague University, K. H. H. Huppert, had suggested that nucleic acids were the carriers of heredity, but proof was not found until the 1940s, in the laboratory of O. T. Avery (1877–1955). The enigma of heredity had to wait for a solution until the discovery of the structure of DNA and RNA (the 'double helix') by Crick and Watson in 1953. That led rapidly to the cracking of the genetic code, and the definition of the hereditary unit in terms of physics, chemistry and cybernetics. Research into heredity had reached the level where molecular genetics was born. The newest experimental model in this research became such organisms as *Neurospora*, bacteria and viruses. Significant developments took place in the biology of the cell, and thus molecular biology arrived on the scene.

Since 1965 many new advances have been made in genetics; it is now possible to manipulate the hereditary unit on the level of cells and molecules (sometimes called genetic engineering). New genetic methods are beginning to be used in the production of organic materials and medicines, in agricultural breeding, and in other spheres; this line of research is finding an outlet in biotechnology. All this had its roots in the discovery of the unit of heredity; yet it is only now that we are beginning to understand the circumstances which led Mendel to his achievement.

In 1932 T. H. Morgan evaluated Mendel's work in the context of the contemporary development of genetics. Though ignorant of the circumstances which led to the classic research described here, he concluded: 'Nevertheless, the genial Abbot's work was not entirely heaven born, but has a background of one hundred years of substantial progress that made it possible for genius to develop to its full measure.' A more complete picture of that progress now permits a fuller appreciation of the modest Moravian scientist whose name is inseparable from the origin and early development of genetics.

Further Reading

Mendel's nine papers on meteorology and his two papers on plant hybridisation were published in the journal of the Brno Natural Science Society between 1863 and 1871. After 1900 the *Pisum* paper was repeatedly published in the original German and in some fifteen other languages. The *Hieracium* paper also appeared many times in German and in nine other languages. The last English translation of the hybridisation papers was published by J. H. Bennett in Edinburgh, in 1965, in a book entitled *Experiments in Plant Hybridization: Gregor Mendel*. In 1966, C. Stern and E. R. Sherwood published a revised English translation of the two hybridisation papers with the support of the American Philosophical Society, New York, under the title *The Origins of Genetics. A Mendel Source-Book*. (Quotations from Mendel's paper in the present study are based on this translation.) More detailed information relating to Mendel and his research activities has been published from 1966 onwards in the series Folia Mendeliana by the Moravian Museum, Brno, Czechoslovakia.

I. Works left unpublished by Mendel

C. Correns, 'Gregor Mendels Briefe an Carl Nägeli, 1866–1873', *Abhandlungen der mathematisch-physikalischen Klasse der königlich-sächsischen Gesellschaft der Wissenschaften* (29:189–265, 1905). An English translation appeared in C. Stern and E. R. Sherwood, *The Origins of Genetics. A Mendel Source-Book*, W. H. Freeman, San Francisco and London, 1966.

II. Mendel's published papers (in order of date)

(*VnV = Verhandlungen des naturforschenden Vereins* (Proceedings of the Natural Science Society), published in Brünn (Brno)).

1853 'Ueber Verwüstung am Gartenrettich durch Raupen (*Botys margaritalis*)', *Verhandlungen zool. bot. Vereins*, Vienna, 3, 116–18

1854 'Brief Mendels an Dir. Kollar über *Bruchus pisi*', *Verhandlungen zool. bot. Vereins*, Vienna, 4, 100–2

1863 'Bemerkungen zu der graphisch-tabellarischen Uebersicht der meteorologischen Verhältnisse von Brünn', *VnV*, 1, 246–9

1864 'Meteorologische Beobachtungen aus Mähren und Schlesien für das Jahr 1863', *VnV*, 2, 99–121

1865 'Meteorologischen Beobachtungen aus Mähren und Schlesien für das Jahr 1864', *VnV*, 3, 209–20

1866 'Versuche über Pflanzen-Hybriden', *VnV*, 4, 3–47

1866 'Meteorologische Beobachtungen aus Mähren und Schlesien für das Jahr 1865', *VnV*, 4, 318–30

1867 'Meteorologische Beobachtungen aus Mähren und Schlesien für das Jahr 1866', *VnV*, 5, 160–72

1870 'Ueber einige aus künstlicher Befruchtung gewonnenen *Hieracium*-Bastarde', *VnV*, 8, 26–31

1870 'Meteorologische Beobachtungen aus Mähren und Schlesien für das Jahr 1869', *VnV*, 8, 131–43

1871 'Die Windhose vom 13. Oktober 1870', *VnV*, 9, 229–46

1877 'Die Bedeutung der Wetterprognosen für Landwirthe', *Mittheilungen der k.k. Mährische–Schlesischen Gesellschaft zur Beförderung des Ackerbaues, der Natur- und der Landeskunde*, p. 385

1879 'Die Grundlage der Wetterprognosen', *Mittheilungen der k.k. Mährisch-Schlesischen Gesellschaft zur Beförderung des Ackerbaues, der Natur- und der Landeskunde*, pp. 29–31.

III. Biographies

1924 H. Iltis, *Gregor Johann Mendel. Leben, Wirken und Wirkung*, J. Springer, Berlin. The first and the most extensive biography, drawing attention to Mendel's origin, birthplace and education. More detailed information deals with Mendel's research into plant hybridisation, his activities in apiculture, horticulture and meteorology, and his position as abbot of the monastery.

1932 *Life of Mendel*, W. W. Norton & Co., New York (English translation of Iltis's monograph). Second English edition, Hafner & Co., New York, 1966.

1943 O. Richter, 'Johann Gregor Mendel wie er wirklich war', *Vnv*, 74, II. 1–262. Some new information relating to Mendel's life and scientific activity. Mendel is presented here more as a religious man and an opponent to Darwin.

1959 H. Sootin, *Gregor Mendel. Father of the Science of Genetics*, The Vanguard Press, Inc., New York. A popular essay on Mendel's life and research activity, mostly drawn from the information of Iltis's monograph.

1965 J. Kříženecký, *Gregor Johann Mendel 1822–1844. Texte und Quellen zu seinem Wirken und Leben*, J. Ambrosius Barth, Leipzig. Original documents in German dealing with Mendel's life and

research activity. Each of the documents is
briefly explained in a commentary.

1966   R. C. Olby, *Origins of Mendelism*, Constable,
       London. Second edition, Schocken Books, New
       York, 1967. Attention is drawn to Mendel's pre-
       cursors in research into plant hybridisation and
       fertilisation.

1975   W. George, *Gregor Mendel and Heredity*, Priory
       Press, London. A popular biography with a series
       of illustrations.

Since 1966 new information on Mendel's life and his
scientific activities has been published annually, mostly
in English, by the Moravian Museum in Brno in the
series Folia Mendeliana.

Besides monographs in English, books on Mendel have
appeared also in German, Japanese and Russian, and to a
lesser extent in other languages. The present study relies
on the monograph by Iltis and the sources mentioned
here.

Index

Index

Mendel, Johann Gregor: (*cont.*):
physics, 22, 23, 28, 30, 32, 83;
and physiology, 28, 37, 42;
knowledge of geology, 27, 66;
activity in meteorology, 27,
82–7, 91; explanation of the
fertilisation of plants, 37, 42,
58; mathematics in his
research, 42, 49, 53, 60, 61;
experiments with other plant
species, 43, 59–67; contact
with Nägeli, 43, 57, 63, 64,
66, 67, 72, 87; views on evolution, 67–71; conflict over
taxation of monastery, 77,
87–9; activity in the Agricultural Society, 77–82;
activity in the Natural Science
Society, 89, 92; interest in
chess, 90; director of the bank,
89; relations with Unger, *see*
Unger
meteorology, 15, 21, 27, 32,
82–7
Mirabilis, 43, 62
Morgan, T. H., 100, 101, 103

Nägeli, C.: quoted by Unger,
40; correspondence with
Mendel, 40, 43, 57, 61, 66, 70,
72, 87; praises Mendel, 64; on
research methods, 71; neglect
of Mendel's theory, 58, 95;
interest in plant hybridisation, 61, 63
Napp, F. C.: supports Mendel,
6, 14, 15, 25–8, 72; interest in
heredity, 13; interest in
natural sciences, 14, 24, 25,
27; activity in agriculture,
12–15; public activities, 14,
74, 76; interest in apiculture,
80–2; defends science in the
monastery, 24, 25
Natural Science Society of Brno:
foundation of, 16; Mendel's
activities in, 16, 77; elucidation of theories by Darwin
and Mendel; 70–1; meteor-
ological activities, 15, 83, 84
Nave, J., 36
Nestler, J. K., 13, 14, 34
Neissl, G., 40, 59, 66, 92, 93

Olexík, P., 83, 84, 91
Olomouc (Olmütz), 13, 14, 22,
30, 74, 83
Opava, 21, 22, 83

Phaseolus, 59, 65, 94
physics: in André's programme,
9; in Zawadski's teaching, 15,
16; Mendel's study of, 22, 23,
28, 30, 32, 83; in Mendel's
research, 53, 57; and the gene
concept, 103
phenotypes, 47, 51, 53
physiology: and heredity, 13,
35, 42, 56, 57, 70; in Mendel's
studies, 28, 37, 42; and hybridisation, 39; in Unger's teaching, 40
Pisum: in Mendel's paper, 37,
40, 59, 63, 70, 94; in Mendel's
research, 42, 44, 45, 53, 73, 87
Pomological Association of
Brno, 11, 13, 14, 18
Pringsheim, N. K., 36–8
Purkyně, J. E., 17, 35, 36, 38

Realschule, 6, 15, 16
recessive, 46
Romanes, G. J., 94
Royal Society of London, 10, 73

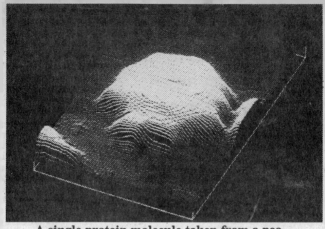

A single protein molecule taken from a pea

Scientists capture molecule on film

By Roger Highfield, Technology Editor

THE FIRST photograph of a single protein molecule in its natural state, shown above, has been taken by British scientists.

The researchers, from the Institute of Food Research at Norwich and Cambridge University, used a scanning tunnelling microscope—a device that can take three-dimensional pictures of surfaces down to the last atom.

The work is to be reported in the International Journal of Biological Macromolecules.

The protein, called vicilin, is found in peas. Under the gaze of the tunnelling microscope "it looks hexagonal or a little like a blancmange," said Dr Victor Morris, who took the picture with Dr Nigel Lambert, Dr Meryn Miles and Dr Mark Welland.

The protein was about one millionth of a centimetre across and about one third that in height. Dr Morris said the team found the ability to take a snap of something so small "astonishing".

The technique could be a boon to protein engineers, who are attempting to redesign natural proteins to help speed chemical reactions in industry.

With the microscope the protein engineers can magnify proteins one million-fold, and directly measure the change in shape caused by their efforts.

Unlike other techniques, notably electron microscopy, the technique does not need a vacuum or any sample preparation such as freezing or drying, so researchers can see the protein in its native conditions.

Though the technique was first developed by IBM Zurich, the scanning microscope used by the researchers was designed and built by a British company, WA Technology of Cambridge.

More Past Masters

Details of a selection of other Past Masters follow. A complete list of Oxford Paperbacks, including the World's Classics, Twentieth-Century Classics, Oxford Shakespeare, Oxford Authors, OPUS, as well as Past Masters series, can be obtained from the General Publicity Department, Oxford University Press, Walton Street, Oxford OX2 6DP.

In the USA, complete lists are available from the Paperbacks Marketing Manager, Oxford University Press, 200 Madison Avenue, New York, NY 10016.

LAMARCK L. J. Jordanova

The great French naturalist Jean-Baptiste de Lamarck has been hailed by some as the founder of evolutionary theory. Others have dismissed him as a minor figure because of his belief in the inheritance of acquired characteristics—a theory now discredited. L. J. Jordanova shows that this theory is peripheral to Lamarck's true achievement. Setting his work in the context of early eighteenth-century science and thought, the author describes his conceptual contribution to modern biology, and shows that much of his work truly establishes him as an important forerunner of Darwin.

Past Masters

LEIBNIZ George MacDonald Ross

Though best known as a philosopher, Gottfried Wilhelm Leibniz was a polymath with many facets to his genius. Besides providing the most detailed account of his life available in English, George MacDonald Ross puts Leibniz's philosophical ideas into perspective by examining them in the light of his work as an alchemist, librarian, diplomat, mining engineer, and historian.

'the book is fresh, stimulating and very informative' R. S. Woolhouse, *Nature*

GALILEO Stillman Drake

In a startling reinterpretation of the evidence, Stillman Drake advances the hypothesis that Galileo's trial and condemnation by the Inquisition was caused not by his defiance of the Church, but by the hostility of contemporary philosophers. Galileo's own beautifully lucid arguments are used to show how his scientific method was utterly divorced from the Aristotelian approach to physics in that it was based on a search not for causes but for laws. Galileo's method was of overwhelming significance for the development of modern physics, and led to a final parting of the ways between science and philosophy.

'an excellent little volume [which] can be warmly recommended, not only to "the educated layman", but more specifically to the student requiring a first introduction to Galileo' *British Journal of the History of Science*

Past Masters

DARWIN Jonathan Howard

Darwin's theory that men's ancestors were apes caused a furore in the scientific world and outside it when *The Origin of Species* was published in 1859. Arguments still rage about the implications of his evolutionary theory, and scepticism about the value of Darwin's contribution to knowledge is widespread. In this analysis of Darwin's major insights and arguments, Jonathan Howard reasserts the importance of Darwin's work for the development of modern biology.

'Jonathan Howard has produced an intellectual *tour de force*, a classic in the genre of popular scientific exposition which will still be read in fifty years' time.' *Times Literary Supplement*

BURKE C. B. Macpherson

This new appreciation of Edmund Burke introduces the whole range of his thought, and offers a novel solution to the main problems it poses. Interpretations of Burke's ideas, which were never systematized in a single work, have varied between apparently incompatible extremes. C. B. Macpherson finds the key to an underlying consistency in Burke's political economy, which, he argues, is a constant factor in Burke's political reasoning.

'Professor Macpherson . . . teases out the strands in Burke's thought so carefully that one comes to understand, not only Burke himself, but his interpreters.' *Times Educational Supplement*

Past Masters

BERKELEY J. O. Urmson

Unlike Dr Johnson in his famous jibe, J. O. Urmson achieves an unusually sympathetic assessment of Berkeley's philosophy by viewing it against a wider intellectual background than is customary. He sees Berkeley's work as a serious critical analysis of the scientific thought of Newton and his predecessors, and of its metaphysical basis; and he gives a clear account of the relationship between Berkeley's metaphysics and his analysis of the concepts of science and common sense.

'Professor Urmson's *Berkeley* is welcome, not just because he makes Berkeley's view that there is no such thing as matter perfectly intelligible and rather persuasive . . . but because he devotes some time to explaining the moral and political positions which Berkeley thought materialism threatened.' *Listener*

PLATO R. M. Hare

Even after twenty-three centuries, Plato's work remains the starting-point for the study of logic, metaphysics, and moral and political philosophy. But though his dialogues retain their freshness and immediacy, they can be difficult to follow. R. M. Hare has provided a short introduction to Plato's work that makes their meaning clear.

'in less than ninety pages makes [this] monumental subject real, intelligible, and interesting' *Times Literary Supplement*

Past Masters

ARISTOTLE Jonathan Barnes

The influence of Aristotle, the prince of philosophers, on the intellectual history of the West is second to none. Jonathan Barnes has written a critical account of his fundamental teachings which places him in his historical context.

'With compressed verve, Jonathan Barnes displays the extraordinary versatility of Aristotle the great systematizing empiricist.' *Sunday Times*

CONFUCIUS Raymond Dawson

Has any individual ever shaped his own country's civilization more thoroughly, or been set up as an example to more of his fellow-countrymen, than Confucius? But what we know about the man himself is vague and shadowy, and the sayings attributed to him may often seem—to the Westerner—obscure, trivial, or banal. Raymond Dawson resolves these paradoxes, showing the contemporary applicability of the sayings, and giving reasons for the strength of their influence throughout the two and a half millennia of their currency.

'This work is to be commended for its quiet and straightforward approach. It is pleasing to have this lucid treatise to recommend to students, and more mature scholars will also find it stimulating.' *British Book News*

Past Masters

PASCAL Alban Krailsheimer

Alban Krailsheimer opens his study of Pascal's life and work with a description of Pascal's religious conversion, and then discusses his literary, mathematical, and scientific achievements, which culminated in the acute analysis of human character and the powerful reasoning of the *Pensées*. He argues that after his conversion Pascal put his previous work in a different perspective and saw his, and in general all, human activity in religious terms.

'Mr Krailsheimer's enthusiasm is eloquent and infectious.'
Observer

HUME A. J. Ayer

A. J. Ayer begins his study of Hume's philosophy with a general account of Hume's life and works, and then discusses his philosophical aims and methods, his theories of perception and self-identity, his analysis of causation, and his treatment of morals, politics, and religion. He argues that Hume's discovery of the basis of causality and his demolition of natural theology were his greatest philosophical achievements.

'Written with predictably impressive skill and verve and graced by a generous selection of Hume's own marvellously elegant ironies, it will no doubt give pleasure as well as instruction to many.'
London Review of Books

Past Masters

LOCKE John Dunn

Although John Locke's *Essay concerning Human Understanding*, in which he set out his theory that men's knowledge reaches them exclusively through their senses, is his best-known and most admired work, it is still curiously misunderstood. By restoring Locke's theory of knowledge to its proper context, John Dunn explains how Locke came to the conclusions he did, and why his views on this fundamental question have so profoundly influenced later generations of philosophers and natural scientists. He also explores Locke's exposition of the liberal values of tolerance and responsible government which was to become the backbone of enlightened European thought in the eighteenth century.

'In eighty lucid and lively pages Dunn has stripped the myths and given us a new key to Locke.' *New Society*

DIDEROT Peter France

Denis Diderot was one of the most brilliant minds of the French Enlightenment, on which his editorship of the *Encyclopedia* gave him a unique vantage-point. In no man were the currents of eighteenth-century thought more intensely present.

This book takes account of the full range of Diderot's writing, from politics to the theatre, from physiology to painting. It stresses the critical impulse which lies at the heart of his work, and pays particular attention to the complexity of his writing, with its manifold and often contradictory voices, and to the nature of his demands on his readers.

'*Diderot* is a provocative study which makes a genuine attempt to give a rapid appraisal of Diderot's breadth. The book never fails to interest.' *Journal of European Studies*

Past Masters

MUHAMMAD Michael Cook

Just over a sixth of the world's population subscribes to the Muslim belief that 'there is no god but God, and Muhammad is His Messenger'. Michael Cook gives an incisive account of the man who inspired this faith, drawing on the traditional Muslim sources to describe Muhammad's life and teaching. He also attempts to stand back from this traditional picture to question how far it is historically justified.

'a moving introduction to the prophet and a very necessary one' Ronald Blythe, *Listener*

THE BUDDHA Michael Carrithers

Michael Carrithers guides us through the complex and sometimes conflicting information that Buddhist texts give about the life and teaching of the Buddha. He discusses the social and political background of India in the Buddha's time, and traces the development of his thought. He also assesses the rapid and widespread assimilation of Buddhism, and its contemporary relevance.

'This is a little book with a lot in it. The author is concerned to discover why the Buddha has so strong an appeal to disillusioned Western thinkers . . . closely-packed original thinking distinguishes this monograph' *The Middle Way*